ACCESS
TO
COLLEGE

MINORITY ACCESS TO COLLEGE

A Ford Foundation Report

By FRED E. CROSSLAND

with a foreword by James E. Cheek

SCHOCKEN BOOKS · NEW YORK

CONTENTS

FOREWORD

AMERICA HAS BEEN committed, in principle, to universal access to higher education for some time. But it was largely in the decade of the 1960's that the implementation of that principle began to engage the serious attention of educators, university governing boards, and political leaders.

The American Council on Education's special report entitled "College and Minority/Poverty Issues" (November 14, 1969) lists more than 190 bibliographical aids, studies, articles, books, and organizational reports dealing with minority participation in higher education.

This study adds to that list. It does so not only by virtue of being one more such study, but more fundamentally by the content and character of its discussion and analysis of the issues. Although a cursory glance at the literature reveals an abundant harvest of facts, opinions, plans, program proposals, etc., there remains a severe famine of hard, realistic analysis.

Largely because of the civil rights movement of the

1960's and the central position of the American campus in many aspects of that struggle, the implications of "universal" access to college began to be related to the struggle of blacks and other Americans.

It is clear that with the beginning of the decade of the 1970's this issue is joined. Blacks and other minorities are becoming increasingly sensitive to the strategic importance of higher education in the context of their current struggle.

This struggle has been labeled a struggle for social justice—a struggle related to civil rights, but one that arouses sufficient distrust in its objectives and tactics and strategies to warrant differentiation. It may be some time yet before the concept of "social justice" becomes established as the appropriate characterization of the ethnic-minority struggle. For many, it is a vague concept, imprecise and ambiguous.

In terms of its objectives, social justice could be defined as *parity and equity in access to and participation in the opportunities, rewards, benefits, and powers of the American society.* The achievement of social justice is not a matter of changing the law—as was the case with civil rights—but rather of changing the structure and character of our society: its attitudes, its practices, its institutions.

What specific strategies and tactics are most appropriate and potentially most effective for reaching that goal have not yet been precisely determined. Mass demonstrations, nonviolent confrontations, and the legal process through the courts clearly were appropriate measures in the civil rights struggle. It is not so clear that these are either appropriate or ultimately effective techniques in achieving social justice.

What is becoming manifest, however, is that social justice is attainable through alteration in the practices of the major American institutions. At the center of these institutions is the institution of higher learning.

One can and should say that the nation's colleges and universities will represent (as they have already) the major focal point in the developing struggle for social justice. In fact, if the definition of social justice given above is the true description of what blacks and other minorities now seek, it can be argued that access to higher education becomes the most strategic and significant (but by no means the only) point at which to aim and launch the attack. For education—and especially higher education—has functioned as the chief instrument of social mobility for every other ethnic group in American society, except for ethnic groups that are not white.

The issue of minority access to college is and becomes one of the dominant issues of the 1970's. Around that issue revolves a host of questions and problems related to the gravity of the racial and ethnic conflict in America, and the answers to those questions as well as the solution to those problems.

Horace Mann wrote: "Education is the great equalizer of the conditions of men; the balance wheel of the social machinery." Mann's observation becomes even more relevant and significant for America in 1971 than it was when he wrote it over a century ago.

Historically within American higher education, with respect to blacks and other minorities, there have existed what have been called an "inequity of quantity" and an "inequity of quality." Both kinds of inequities have resulted in significant segments of the national population not sharing in and profiting from the benefits and rewards of higher education, which makes possible equitable participation in the larger society's social, economic, cultural, and political life. That is, inequities in access to higher educational opportunity have resulted in inequities in access to and participation in the American society as a whole.

For unprivileged and disadvantaged minorities the question of accessibility to and success in collegiate-level opportunity is more than the question of obtaining a "union card" or "passport" for full entry into American life. For such groups it is more fundamentally the acquisition of that competence that higher learning is supposed to, and presumably designed to, produce and develop.

After obtaining the degree—the formal recognition of having met all the requirements and being granted all the "rights and privileges thereunto pertaining"—the acid test is one's ability to function competently in a society where achievement, effectiveness, and ability are supposed to dictate the degree and extent of one's participation in the rewards, benefits, and powers available in the society.

For this reason we must regard both the *quality* of the opportunity and the *number* of those who have such opportunity as basically *existential* and not simply *idealistic* considerations. For blacks and other minorities, it is not merely a question of succeeding, but more fundamentally a question of surviving in an intensely competitive and open society.

This study of minority access to college brings to the forefront many issues and questions that have been the subjects of other discussions. But two issues are particularly highlighted for further investigation, analysis, and discussion. These are: (1) the number of black and other minority students currently enrolled in higher education; and (2) the role of the traditionally black institutions (TBI's) in increasing minority access to and successful participation in the college experience.

The first issue could be easily resolved with a careful and painstaking gathering of the data. It is primarily a statistical question, but we badly need to know more precisely than we do now where the nation is with respect to the percentage of the eligible college-age population enjoying or not enjoying the fruits of higher learning. What is abundantly clear, however, is that black students are grossly underrepresented at a time when they need to be overrepresented, and that the nation has to devote substantially more resources and facilities—rather than less— to the education of these youth.

The second issue is not so easily settled. For the present and future place of TBI's in the nation's pluralistic educational system involves the quality of higher education as well as the number of students who have access to it.

It is an issue that has to be rationally discussed and dispassionately evaluated. Bound up in that issue are a number of others which are inherent and essential factors in the overall issue of the ultimate achievement of social justice.

With respect to the quantitative question, the issue of the TBI's is largely one of whether these institutions are capable of accommodating additional numbers of students. While this debate proceeds, the enrollment of these colleges has been steadily increasing; their resources have not kept pace.

The second question is, What constitutes "quality" education? What ought to be the nature and character of the collegiate experience to which blacks and other minorities have access? What considerations of social policy and national goals dictate these colleges' continuance or their reduction in numbers or their being phased out altogether? What are the social and political consequences of their continuance?

Although there has been a plethora of studies, surveys, and reports on this group of institutions recently, beginning with McGrath's report in 1965, followed by the Southern Regional Education Board report in 1967, the Jencks-Riesman survey in 1967, the Carnegie Commission report in 1970, and the report of the President's Commission on Campus Unrest, there remains the need—indeed the urgency—to engage this issue and its concomitant considerations in the light of the current situation that the "black revolution" has created.

In 1965, McGrath could state that if his report did nothing else, "it should establish the fact that, except at the topmost level of excellence represented by a few celebrated institutions, the Negro institutions run the entire gamut of quality within American higher education." Two years later, Riesman and Jencks were to dispute that contention in their characterization of Negro colleges as constituting the "disaster area of American higher education." While the judgments represented by these two reports may be based on a host of subjective considerations, the "facts" of the situation can be established by more objective means based upon accepted criteria.

It was not the purpose of the present study to treat the question of the TBI's analytically or in depth. But it does furnish the information and some of the considerations that are important for further study and discussion.

Minority Access to College is a controversial statement. It should be, because it deals with a controversial issue. It adds substantially to the level of the national discourse on issues surrounding the education of black and minority youth. And the report makes it very clear that this nation —all sectors of our society at all levels—must substantially advance social justice for our minorities by supporting their access to higher education and by supporting the black institutions. For these youth and these institutions are among the nation's outstanding neglected resources.

JAMES E. CHEEK

Howard University
Washington, D.C.
February 1971

PREFACE

IN 1966 the Ford Foundation established the Office of Special Projects within its Education and Research Division. Its assignment: to study, seek solutions for, and support selected efforts to cope with the higher education problems of America's underrepresented racial and ethnic minorities. The Foundation had for several years previous been deeply concerned about a variety of educational and social disabilities suffered by minorities, and it had assisted many approaches to dealing with these problems. The creation of a new office reflected the Foundation's commitment to do more and to focus resources and staff attention on the post-secondary educational problems of Black Americans, Mexican Americans, Puerto Ricans, and American Indians. It was clear then as now that a college education and credentials are important prerequisites for full participation in the American economy and society. If minority youth could not get into and through institutions of higher learning, their disadvantaged competitive positions probably would continue.

This report deals with one aspect of the work of the Office of Special Projects—that is, the problem of getting into college. It does not suggest that many long-standing inequities at the point of entry have now been removed. It attempts only to describe where America presently stands in its quest for equal and fair access to college, and to indicate the dimensions and complexities of the unfinished task.

In the course of our work, my colleagues and I visited scores of colleges and universities throughout the United States, and we met and talked with hundreds of minority students, faculty members, college presidents and other educational administrators, government officials, and community leaders. The comments, insights, reports, and statistical data they shared with us have been essential ingredients in the study that follows.

The reader should remind himself frequently that the statistical data presented on the following pages are not exact, but rather are carefully developed estimates and extrapolations based on many different (and sometimes differing) sources. My own experience as a professor, educational administrator, university dean of admissions, and Ford Foundation staff member has persuaded me that demographic data and enrollment statistics invariably are imprecise and should be interpreted with care. This I have tried to do; the reader is urged to do likewise.

I am deeply indebted to many people for their helpful advice in the preparation of this report. Dr. James E.

Cheek, President of Howard University, not only contributed a thoughtful and provocative foreword, but also read an early draft of the manuscript and offered valued suggestions. This report also benefited immeasurably from careful reading by—and perceptive and constructive criticisms from—Alexander Heard, Chancellor of Vanderbilt University; Kermit Gordon, President of Brookings Institution; Vivian W. Henderson, President of Clark College; Kenneth B. Clark, President of Metropolitan Applied Research Center, Inc.; and S. A. Kendrick, Executive Associate of the College Entrance Examination Board. Many of my Ford Foundation colleagues offered suggestions that enhanced the style and increased the accuracy of the manuscript. Any remaining errors of fact or judgment are my responsibility alone.

Seeking to shed some light on a complex problem and to describe objectively where we now stand, this report is intended to help us move one step closer toward the justice and equity we profess to seek.

1
MINORITY COLLEGE STUDENTS

AMERICAN HIGHER EDUCATION is an extraordinary enterprise which includes eight million students and half a million teachers and administrators at nearly 2,600 colleges and universities. This effort is unmatched by any other country in the quality of its research and teaching, in the size of its enrollment, in the proportion of the nation's youth which it serves, and in the diversity of its institutions and offerings.

During the last one hundred years, America's collegiate enrollment has doubled approximately every ten or twelve years, but this phenomenal expansion can be attributed only in small part to the growth of the total population. Far more important has been a dramatic increase in the proportion of young people attending college. A century ago, barely 3 or 4 per cent of Americans continued their formal, institutionalized training beyond secondary school; today 50 per cent do so. The growth curve shows no sign of leveling off, and serious attention now is being given to the possibility of universal higher education in America.[1]

3

The attainment of 50 per cent participation at the point of entry is a remarkable achievement, but one which is a source of no satisfaction and much bitterness to many of those among the half not being served. Social and economic mobility (which always is assumed to be upward) increasingly appears to be dependent upon collegiate credentials, and hence the educationally disfranchised are persuaded—with good reason—that they are denied access to equitable rewards, status, and social participation.

At the beginning of the 1970's the most intense pressure for expanded opportunities for higher education comes from Black Americans, Mexican Americans, Puerto Ricans, and American Indians—four groups that in recent years have become ever more vocal, visible, impatient, and militant. During the 1960's each of these minority groups made substantial enrollment increases, in large measure as a result of the accelerated civil rights movement and increased white consciousness of historic inequities and the brutalizing impact of racial prejudice. But minority expectations predictably outraced majority performance, and in 1970 each of the four groups was still substantially underrepresented on America's campuses.

Conditions have been changing and will continue to change so rapidly that it is difficult to describe the situation with precision. Growing minority militancy and conservative counterreaction in the late 1960's often raised the temperature but reduced the illumination. Colleges and universities, which long had taken pride in being citadels of reasoned discourse, themselves became the settings for shouting matches and violence. Administrators were constrained to make admission-policy decisions affecting minorities without adequate statistical data and without full realization of the financial, educational, and curricular implications of their decisions.

The analyses that follow attempt to set forth objectively and quantitatively the major issues related to pressures for increased higher educational opportunities for Black Americans, Mexican Americans, Puerto Ricans, and American Indians. Particular attention is given to (a) the changing character and dimensions of minority participation in higher learning, (b) the major barriers to college faced by minority students, and (c) the methods by which some of those barriers are being removed. America's colleges and universities can help to mend or tear the fragile social fabric by the policies they adopt and implement. They have both the opportunity and the responsibility to deal judiciously and compassionately with these complicated circumstances, but to do so they need precise information about the underrepresented minorities.

The Problems of Counting

MOST DATA ABOUT American higher education are subject to question, because definitions and categories are not uniformly employed. Enrollment statistics are especially difficult to accept uncritically because the terms "student" and "college" are subject to many interpretations.[2]

A roster of post-secondary educational institutions, for example, may or may not include technical institutes, junior colleges, correspondence schools, theological seminaries, and a confusing and uneven variety of trade schools along with more conventional, degree-granting, four-year colleges and universities. Occasionally, data are restricted to institutions accredited by regional associations.

Simply counting students is surprisingly complicated. Some published enrollment figures may be based on a head count of all students. Others may include full-time students only, and still others may cite a number of "full-time equivalents" by counting part-timers as fractions of students. Some statistics may be limited to matriculants— i.e., formal degree candidates. Others may include "special students" who enroll for one or two courses but who are not following prescribed curricula. Some may be limited to resident students, and others may include extension, correspondence, and television students. Some reports may be for the first day of classes; others may be for a period some weeks later after considerable attrition has taken place.

Even less precise are all statistics seeking to classify people by race or ethnic background. Racial data inevitably are suspect because they depend upon subjective self-identification or the eye of a fallible observer, rather than upon objective criteria. As a result, any attempt to count minority-group college students is likely to produce compounded imprecision.

Minority-student identifications are difficult to secure for a variety of reasons. For example, some liberal white supporters of racial integration and cultural assimilation have long struggled to be color-blind and now find it distasteful to label individuals. Some university administrators simply refuse to respond to questionnaires seeking "sensitive" data which might, if released, disturb campus equilibrium. At many institutions racial censuses are a voluntary part of the registration procedure, and as a result the published figures may be nothing more than extensions of unrepresentative samples. At some universities it appears that students gleefully disrupt "the system" by providing false information, mutilating punched cards, and confusing the computer.

There are three major sources of recent national black-enrollment data: the Bureau of the Census; the Office for Civil Rights in the Department of Health, Education, and Welfare; and research reports published by the American Council on Education. The census figures are based upon a detailed analysis of a survey of 50,000 representative households rather than a national head count.[3] The Office for Civil Rights collects estimates and reports from many, but not all, colleges and universities.[4] The American Council on Education's figures are limited to new freshmen and are based on questionnaires received from students at a representative sample of higher institutions.[5]

The three systems of data collection leave much to be desired, and the differences between their results are large and sometimes difficult to reconcile. The census figures—expressed as numbers of students—may be inflated because low-income, minority respondents probably tend to define "student" and "college" generously when they report about their own families. On the other hand, the Office for Civil Rights surveys may be too low because some institutions are delinquent in submitting data and others provide information suffering from one or more of the campus shortcomings and distortions described above. The American Council figures—expressed as percentages —vary considerably from year to year and may be off target because some student respondents refuse to classify themselves in logical or expected fashion.

In the absence of consistent and precise data, it has been necessary to reconcile substantial differences in published figures and make educated guesses based upon personal observations, analyses of trends over a number of years, and conversations with educational administrators throughout the country. All the data presented below should be treated as reasonable approximations. Errors of as much as 10 per cent are entirely possible.

Minorities and the Total Population

TOTAL POPULATION figures for 1970 were approximately as follows:

Black Americans	23,550,000	11.5%
Mexican Americans	5,000,000	2.4
Puerto Ricans	1,500,000	0.7
American Indians	700,000	0.4
Sub-total	30,750,000	15.0
All others	174,250,000	85.0
Total	205,000,000	100.0%

The minority figures may be too low. Some minority spokesmen have alleged that their groups regularly are undercounted in the official U.S. census because of failures to reach all of the poor, the non-English-speaking, those residing in deteriorated urban slums, and migrant workers. The official 1960 black-population figure of 18,800,000 was as much as 5,000,000 short of the true figure according to some Negro leaders, and questions about the accuracy of the 1970 census were raised by them even before the counting had been completed. The census estimate of the black population in January 1969 was 22,331,000,

10

and it was reported that it had been increasing about 2 per cent annually during the 1960's.[6] That would put the census figure at about 23,000,000 in mid-1970. The estimate employed here is slightly higher.

There are sufficient data about Black Americans in other periods of history to permit some demographic comparisons.[7] The first census in 1790 counted nearly 700,000 blacks—about 20 per cent of the total population. The ending of slave importation and increased white migration combined to reduce the black percentage to 14.3 by 1860. Since 1900 the percentage has changed little, staying near 11. Current census projections, however, indicate that the 1980 percentage will be 12.4 (28 million black people) and that it will rise to 13.6 (35 million) in 1990.[8] It is expected that during the next two decades the black population will continue to grow at a more rapid rate than the total population. One basis for this prediction is the fact that blacks are younger than whites: the median age of blacks is 21, while that of whites is 29. Also significant is the fact that blacks constitute 15 per cent of all Americans under the age of 5.

The Mexican American population is difficult to define, locate, and study. It is estimated that 85 per cent of the members of this group reside in five Southwestern states, with major concentrations in Texas and California.[9]

The Puerto Rican figures given above are only for residents of the continental United States, more than half of whom probably live in the New York metropolitan area. There is considerable traffic between the States and the island of Puerto Rico (which has a population of approximately 2.5 million), and this makes it difficult to be sure that there is no double counting of people. Virtually all of the migration from the island to the mainland has occurred since World War II.

Obtaining population figures for American Indians poses special problems.[10] Government agencies sometimes publish statistics that include only Indians on reservations —a number that may be little more than half the actual national total. A non-governmental estimate in 1968 put the total at 600,000, with 380,000 living on reservations. The largest concentrations were in Arizona (85,000), Oklahoma (65,000), New Mexico (57,000), Alaska (50,-000), California (40,000), and North Carolina (40,-000).[11] Non-reservation Indians are not easily identified and counted, but it is assumed that a growing proportion of them are moving to, and being "lost" or assimilated in, large metropolitan areas.

Minority College Enrollment

THE ESTIMATED TOTAL higher education enrollment in the fall of 1970 was as follows:

Black Americans	470,000	5.8%
Mexican Americans	50,000	0.6
Puerto Ricans	20,000	0.3
American Indians	4,000	0.1
Sub-total	544,000	6.8
All others	7,506,000	93.2
Total	8,050,000	100.0%

Broad and inclusive definitions of "student" and "college" have been employed in making this estimate.[12] The figures for the minorities are more likely to be too high than too low.

The one enrollment estimate which is most subject to question is that for Black Americans. The Census Bureau reported total black enrollments of 234,000 in 1964, 434,000 in 1968,[13] and 492,000 in 1969.[14] A simple projection of that five-year growth curve would provide a 1970 black enrollment of nearly 560,000. For reasons explained above, the census figures may be too high, and

13

accordingly they have been reduced by more than 15 per cent to the 1970 estimate used here (470,000).

The enrollment of all four minorities tends to be disproportionately concentrated in the early undergraduate years, both because minority freshman enrollments have been increasing recently[15] and because academic survival rates continue to be lower for minority students than for others, and hence relatively few of them are able to complete baccalaureate studies and embark on graduate and professional training.

Minority Underrepresentation

THE DEGREE OF underrepresentation of each of the four minority groups may be determined by computing the relationship between each minority's estimated enrollment and its estimated total population. The ratios (expressed as percentages) are as follows:

	% of population enrolled
Black Americans	2.0
Mexican Americans	1.0
Puerto Ricans	1.3
American Indians	0.6
Sub-total	1.8
All others	4.3
Total	3.9

In order to achieve proportional representation, the enrollment of minorities would have to be increased to the point where their ratios were the same as that given above for "all others" (4.3%). To reach that goal immediately:

the estimated black enrollment in 1970 would have to be increased by 543,000 (from 470,000 to 1,013,000) —an increase of 116 per cent

the estimated Mexican American enrollment in 1970 would have to be increased by 165,000 (from 50,000 to 215,000)—an increase of 330 per cent

the estimated Puerto Rican enrollment in 1970 would have to be increased by 45,000 (from 20,000 to 65,000)—an increase of 225 per cent

the estimated American Indian enrollment in 1970 would have to be increased by 26,000 (from 4,000 to 30,000)—an increase of 650 per cent.

The four minority groups, taken together, were underrepresented in the 1970–71 academic year by 779,000 students. Instead of the actual 544,000 minority students there should have been 1,323,000 matriculants to achieve statistical parity. The addition of 779,000 students to America's higher education effort would increase the total collegiate enterprise by 9.7 per cent (from 8,050,000 to 8,829,000 students).

The foregoing estimates of current minority underrepresentation would be even higher if the college-age group were used as a base rather than the total population. The median age of each of the four minority groups is considerably lower than that of the rest of the population. Although Black Americans, Mexican Americans, Puerto Ricans, and American Indians constitute an estimated 15 per cent of the total population, it is likely that they represent 17 or 18 per cent of all Americans between the ages of 18 and 24. Thus, the numbers of additional minority students needed to achieve proportional representation are conservative if consideration is limited to the appropriate age group.

At no time in American history have all ethnic, racial, religious, economic, and social groups been proportionately represented in higher education enrollment. It is impossible to secure precise data for two centuries of changing American experience, but there have been (and in some cases, still are) obvious examples of underrepresented and overrepresented segments of society. Among the underrepresented have been women, residents of the American South, rural inhabitants, Roman Catholics (until recently, at least), people from eastern and southern European stock, Protestant fundamentalists, blacks, and children of unskilled workers. On the other hand, the overrepresented have included men, urban residents, Jews (especially in the last three or four decades), Chinese- and Japanese-Americans, people of Anglo-Saxon stock, and children of professionals. The reasons for these phenomena are varied and complex. It seems clear, however, that in the cases cited above (with the probable exception of the male-female enrollment disparity) the underrepresented tended to have below-average incomes and the overrepresented enjoyed above-average incomes.

It is unlikely that there are many, if any, advocates of *exact* proportional representation on America's campuses or of *precise* admission quotas to achieve that objective. On the other hand, serious questions have been appropriately raised in a society which professes to be "open" but that continues, consciously or otherwise, to permit unequal access to one of its prime agencies for individual social and economic advancement. Black Americans, Mexican Americans, Puerto Ricans, and American Indians are raising those questions now.

Minority Freshmen in 1970

THE FIGURES cited above refer to *total* higher education enrollment and *total* numerical underrepresentation. The goal of enrollment parity could not and would not be reached "instantly," but rather would have to be achieved over a period of time by increasing the number of minority freshmen and maintaining parity at the point of entry.

The estimated composition of the actual 1970 freshman class was as follows:

Black Americans	132,000	6.6%
Mexican Americans	18,000	0.9
Puerto Ricans	8,000	0.4
American Indians	2,000	0.1
Sub-total	160,000	8.0
All others	1,840,000	92.0
Total	2,000,000	100.0%

If the 1970 national freshman class accurately reflected the composition of the *total* population and if the number of "all other" freshmen remained unchanged, the distribution would have been as follows:

19

Black Americans	249,000	11.5%
Mexican Americans	52,000	2.4
Puerto Ricans	15,000	0.7
American Indians	9,000	0.4
Sub-total	325,000	15.0
All others	1,840,000	85.0
Total	2,165,000	100.0%

In other words, a major step toward ending minority underrepresentation in American higher education in the course of four or five years would have been taken if

the number of 1970 black freshmen were increased by 89 per cent or 117,000 (from 132,000 to 249,000)

the number of 1970 Mexican American freshmen were increased by 189 per cent or 34,000 (from 18,000 to 52,000)

the number of 1970 Puerto Rican freshmen were increased by 88 per cent or 7,000 (from 8,000 to 15,000)

the number of 1970 American Indian freshmen were increased by 350 per cent or 7,000 (from 2,000 to 9,000).

Three conditions would have to be met to achieve parity in total enrollment over a period of time. First, minority freshmen would have to continue to constitute 15 per cent of the total national freshman class in future years. Second, the academic attrition of undergraduate minority students would have to be no higher than that for "all other" students. Third, minority students would have to constitute 15 per cent of the total enrollment in graduate and professional schools.

Here again it should be pointed out that the 15 per cent goal may be too low; if only the college-age group were considered, the figure should be 17 or 18 per cent. Nevertheless, the point is clear: the 1970 minority freshman enrollment would need to be more than doubled in order to achieve proportional representation on America's campuses.

2
BLACK AMERICANS IN COLLEGE

THE MINORITY POPULATION and enrollment data presented above merely seek to describe the situation in 1970. Patterns have been changing over the years, of course, and an analysis of the past would be helpful in understanding the present and laying plans for the future. However, the lack of precise and consistent information about Mexican American, Puerto Rican, and American Indian college students makes it difficult to undertake a review of these groups. It is likely that their enrollment figures were so small until very recently that comparisons with earlier decades would have little utility. On the other hand, some limited historical information about black enrollment is available.[16] Furthermore, the existence of a group of colleges especially created for black students has opened unusual opportunities for Black Americans and invites careful study.

The Growth of Black Collegiate Enrollment

BLACKS, BY far the largest racial minority, have been virtually excluded from all levels of formal education for the greater part of American history. Throughout most of the South before the Civil War, the schooling of slaves was prohibited by law, and only a very small proportion of blacks were taught to read and write by their masters. According to contemporary reports shortly before the Civil War, only 2 per cent of the slaves in the Southwest and slightly more than 1 per cent of those in Georgia were literate.[17] Educational opportunities for blacks in the ante-bellum "free" states probably were somewhat better, but equitable treatment was almost unknown.

In view of these circumstances, it is remarkable that there was a small but nonetheless impressive number of Northern and Southern black poets, authors, teachers, and professionals before the Civil War, and that there reportedly were "28 persons of acknowledged Negro descent" who were graduated with baccalaureate degrees from American higher institutions in all the years before 1860.[18]

The post-Civil War period witnessed a flurry of educational activity on behalf of the newly freed slaves.[19]

Most, but by no means all, of this effort was initiated, financially supported, and controlled by whites, the vast majority of whom were church-connected Northerners. However, the accomplishments of black self-help, despite overwhelming odds, were extraordinary and should not be overlooked. Between 1865 and 1900 hundreds of Negro educational enterprises called institutes, academies, colleges, and universities were established. The great majority of these were located in the Southern and border states, but some were in the North. In their earliest years, almost all of these institutions were largely elementary and secondary schools, but a score or more did have collegiate departments.[20] (This was not unlike the situation in hundreds of predominantly white "colleges" at that time.) By 1876, blacks reportedly had received a total of 208 baccalaureate and 96 professional degrees from both black and white colleges. It is likely that many of those early baccalaureate degree recipients attended either Lincoln University (Pennsylvania) or Wilberforce University (Ohio), two of the earliest predominantly Negro institutions and both established before the Civil War.[21]

It is estimated that all of the twenty to thirty Negro colleges operating in 1895 had together produced 1,151 graduates up to that time. Perhaps an additional 194 Black Americans received degrees from white colleges during the period from 1865 to 1895. Of the latter, 75 were graduates of Oberlin College in Ohio.

By 1900, 34 educational enterprises founded for Negroes were reported to be offering collegiate training. Somewhat more than 2,000 blacks had received degrees by

that date, and between 700 and 800 were currently enrolled in white and Negro higher institutions. In 1916 a
survey by federal education authorities disclosed that only
33 out of 653 public and private educational institutions
for blacks were teaching any subjects of college grade.[22]
It is likely, however, that those 33 Negro colleges enrolled
80–90 per cent of all blacks then in higher education.

Information about total black collegiate enrollment
through all the years before 1920 is so fragmentary and
questionable that it is of little value for purposes of com-
parison. For 1920–60, such data as are available deal
with Negro colleges only and have little to say about blacks
in other institutions. Fifty-seven of the larger Negro colleges were reported to have the following combined enrollments in the years indicated:

1919	8,193
1929	16,392
1939	29,313
1949	51,689
1953	49,153

These data obviously have limited value in determining
national black enrollment because (a) there is no assurance
that only college-grade students were included, (b) not
all of the Negro colleges provided information, and (c)
there are no clues about blacks who may have been enrolled elsewhere.

Other estimates help to suggest the range of total black
collegiate enrollment over the years. One source, based
on the U.S. Bureau of Education *Bulletin,* reported that

in 1916 there were 107,203 black students of all grades enrolled in 747 black institutions; of the total enrollment, however, 80,376 were in elementary schools, 24,186 in secondary schools, and only 2,641 in colleges.[23] Ten years later there reportedly were 12,000 black students in 79 Negro colleges.[24] And in 1932, 22,917 students were counted at 109 Negro colleges located in nineteen states and the District of Columbia.[25] Another source, however, provided a much higher estimate the very next year: the 1933 national figure was put at 38,000 black students, with all but perhaps a thousand attending Negro colleges.[26]

Despite the lack of firm and consistent data, it is possible to make the following rough guesses about total national black collegiate enrollment during the twentieth century:

1900	700–800
1910	3,000–4,000
1920	6,000–8,000
1930	20,000–25,000
1940	45,000–50,000
1950	95,000–105,000
1960	195,000–205,000
1970	470,000

The growth of black enrollment obviously has been extraordinary. The rate of increase has been considerably greater than that of the total American population, the total black population, or the total enrollment in higher education. It must be remembered, however, that the base figures for black enrollment at the beginning of the twentieth century were distressingly low. Blacks then constituted less than 2 per cent of all college students. Now they are approaching 6 per cent, but the current figure should be nearly doubled to achieve parity.

Finally, the remarkable growth in the college attendance of blacks was possible only because of an educational achievement with few parallels in history. In 1870, at least 81 per cent of all Black Americans who were ten years or older were illiterate. By 1930, two generations later, that figure was down to 16 per cent,[27] and by 1970 it had been reduced even further.

The Distribution of Black College Students

CURRENT STATISTICS about total black population and enrollment confirm the fact that significant demographic changes have been taking place at an accelerating pace during recent decades. The following trends merit special consideration:

1. *The proportion of Black Americans living in the South has been declining.* On the eve of the Civil War, 92 per cent of all blacks resided in the South.[28] By 1900, that percentage had changed only slightly to 90. By 1940, however, the figure was down to 77 per cent, and it continued to decline to 68 per cent in 1950, 60 per cent in 1960, and 52 per cent in 1970. During the period 1900–1970, while the percentage of Black Americans in the South fell from 90 to 52, it increased in the North Central area from 6 to 22, in the Northeast from 4 to 18, and in the West from less than 1 to 8. These changes obviously affected the racial composition of the South. In 1900, approximately 33 per cent of all Southerners were black; in 1970 the figure was 19 per cent.[29]

2. *The black population movement, North and South, has been away from rural areas and small towns and toward the central cities of metropolitan areas.*[30] Between 1950 and 1970, the percentage of Black Americans residing in central cities increased from about 43 to 55; in metropolitan suburbs it changed slightly from 13 to 15; and in rural areas it declined from 44 to 30.[31]

3. *Black enrollment, along with that of all other students, has been growing rapidly in the public sector of higher education but has remained fairly steady in the private sector.*[32] Total American college and university enrollment in 1950 was equally divided between private and public institutions. In 1970, enrollment in the public sector constituted nearly 75 per cent of the total. About 80 per cent of all blacks enrolled in 1970 attended public institutions.

4. *The proportion of new black freshmen (and of all other new freshmen) beginning their study in two-year rather than four-year colleges has been growing rapidly.*[33] The increasing urbanization of Black Americans makes it likely that public, urban, junior community colleges will become the most important point for their entry into postsecondary education. In 1970, more than half of all black freshmen were in two-year colleges.

5. *Despite reluctant compliance and stubborn resistance in some places, de jure and de facto segregation in higher education has been eroding.*[34] As a result, black students now have more institutional options available. They are no longer effectively restricted to attendance at

Negro colleges, and a growing proportion of them are selecting—and being selected by—non-Negro institutions.

As a result of these long-term trends, Black American college students now are distributed widely, both geographically and according to type of institution. It is virtually impossible to secure an exact count of the numbers of colleges and universities classified by type and level of instruction,[35] and racial enrollment data are equally difficult to obtain. Nevertheless, reasonably accurate estimates can be made about the distribution of 470,000 black students among 2,600 colleges and universities. The pattern in 1970 was about as follows:

Colleges	Black students	Distribution
Traditionally Black Institutions		
51 private senior	53,050	11.3%
11 private two-year	2,950	0.6
34 public senior	102,025	21.7
4 public two-year	1,975	0.4
100	160,000	34.0
All Other Institutions		
1,150 private senior	35,000	7.5
250 private two-year	2,000	0.4
400 public senior	122,000	26.0
700 public two-year	151,000	32.1
2,500	310,000	66.0
2,600	470,000	100.0%

The fact that almost two-thirds of all black students in 1970 were enrolled in other than traditionally black institutions (TBI's) represents a significant change in less than a decade. As recently as 1964, more than half of all blacks were in TBI's.

Despite the shift to non-Negro colleges in both South and North, the TBI's in 1970 were overwhelmingly "black" while "all other institutions" continued to have student bodies in which blacks constituted very small minorities. The following are estimates:

Colleges	Total enrollment	Black enrollment	Per cent black
Traditionally Black Institutions			
51 private senior	55,000	53,050	96.5%
11 private two-year	3,000	2,950	98.3
34 public senior [36]	108,000	102,025	94.5
4 public two-year	2,000	1,975	98.8
100	168,000	160,000	95.2
All Other Institutions			
1,150 private senior	1,720,000	35,000	2.0
250 private two-year	250,000	2,000	0.8
400 public senior	3,990,000	122,000	3.1
700 public two-year	1,922,000	151,000	7.9
2,500	7,882,000	310,000	3.9
2,600	8,050,000	470,000	5.8%

It is estimated that in 1970 there were 132,000 new black freshmen. No precise figures are available, but it is likely that they were distributed among the 2,600 higher institutions about as follows:

Colleges	Black freshmen	Distri- bution
Traditionally Black Institutions		
51 private senior	12,800	9.7%
11 private two-year	1,200	0.9
34 public senior	25,600	19.4
4 public two-year	900	0.7
100	40,500	30.7
All Other Institutions		
1,150 private senior	6,000	4.5
250 private two-year	500	0.4
400 public senior	18,500	14.0
700 public two-year	66,500	50.4
2,500	91,500	69.3
2,600	132,000	100.0%

It is important to restate that data in the three foregoing tables are not based on verifiable head counts, but
rather are estimates drawn from a variety of sources. Despite the inevitable imprecision, however, they do provide
a reasonably accurate picture of blacks on American
campuses in 1970.

The Traditionally Black Institutions

ANY ANALYSIS of the opportunities for black access to higher education must give careful attention to the black colleges.[37] Until recently they provided virtually the only avenues for post-secondary study, and in 1970 they continued to enroll at least one-third of all Black American college students. For some time to come, they obviously will play a substantial role for America's largest underrepresented minority.

It is no easy task to identify, classify, and label black institutions of higher learning in America. Until late in the 1960's it was conventional to distinguish between "predominantly Negro" and "predominantly white" colleges and universities. But growing minority self-consciousness and militancy led to the gradual substitution of the word "black" for "Negro." Meanwhile, changing enrollment patterns encouraged the abandonment of the word "predominantly" in favor of "founded for," "historically," or "traditionally." By 1970 it seemed to be most accurate and acceptable to distinguish between "traditionally black" and "all other" institutions.

The exact number of traditionally black institutions

(TBI's) is subject to question. The author of a careful study in 1963[38] identified 123 such colleges and universities, including 72 under private sponsorship (49 senior and 23 junior) and 51 under public control (35 senior and 16 junior). The best count in 1970 appeared to be 100, which included 62 private institutions (51 senior and 11 junior) and 38 public institutions (34 senior and 4 junior). With the exception of two in Pennsylvania and two in Ohio, all the TBI's were located in Southern and border states.

For the most part, the reduction in the number of TBI's from 123 to 100 during the years between 1963 and 1970 was the result of mergers, closings, conversions of junior to senior colleges, and the desegregation of some of the formerly all-black public community colleges.[39] It is of interest to note that two of the public senior *historically* Negro colleges (Bluefield State College and West Virginia State College) so increased their white enrollments during the 1960's that they no longer were *predominantly* Negro colleges in 1970, and in some contexts preferred not to be classified with the TBI's. On the other hand, there were perhaps twenty or more new two-year and four-year public institutions in major cities in the North, Midwest, and West in 1970 that were *predominantly* black (Federal City College in Washington, D.C., for example) but obviously should not be included among the *traditionally* black institutions.

Confusion sometimes arises because the combined enrollment of TBI's is mistakenly assumed to be totally Black American. In fact, some of the TBI's—notably Howard

University in Washington, D.C., Lincoln University in Pennsylvania, and Lincoln University in Missouri—enroll significant numbers of white and foreign students. In all TBI enrollment analyses, it is important to distinguish among counts of (*a*) *all* students, (*b*) all *black* students (which ordinarily includes Africans, West Indians, and others), and (*c*) all *Black American* students.

During the 1960's the traditionally black institutions served a diminishing proportion of the total national Black American enrollment. In 1960, the TBI's probably enrolled 65–70 per cent of the total. The author of a 1963 study reported that "Negro colleges enroll over half of all Negroes attending the nation's institutions of higher education," [40] but no precise percentage was given. According to the Bureau of the Census, the TBI's in 1964 enrolled 51 per cent of all Black American students (120,000 out of 234,000); by 1968, however, that figure had been reduced to 36 per cent (156,000 out of 434,000). [41] The estimates appearing on the preceding pages put the percentage at 34 in 1970 (160,000 out of 470,000). During the years between 1964 and 1970

total Black American enrollment increased 101 per cent (from 234,000 to 470,000)

total Black American enrollment in TBI's increased 33 per cent (from 120,000 to 160,000)

total Black American enrollment in all other institutions increased 172 per cent (from 114,000 to 310,000)

83 per cent of the national increase in Black American enrollment took place in *other* than traditionally black institutions.

The impact of these recent developments and the likelihood that this trend will continue [42] are matters of grave concern to all associated with the traditionally black institutions.[43] For years their case for obtaining support from public[44] and private sources was based on the argument that they were the primary educational resource for Black Americans, but current statistics clearly indicate that conditions have been changing and suggest that old arguments and claims no longer are valid.[45]

The situation is much more complicated than the casual observer might suspect. Obviously the stakes are high for the TBI's, but the claims of competing interests tend to confuse rather than enlighten the general public.[46] TBI spokesmen, for example, can point out quite accurately that their institutions have produced most of America's black college graduates; but that is the result of past enrollment patterns which now have changed markedly.[47] TBI's can also justifiably claim that they are the most important educational institutions for *Southern* blacks; but soon a majority of Black Americans will be living outside of the South.[48] Some TBI advocates correctly point out that they enroll a majority of the black baccalaureate candidates; but that distinction is achieved only by disregarding the burgeoning two-year college enrollment, which increasingly will include Black Americans who plan to transfer to baccalaureate programs in senior colleges.[49] Nor can the TBI's base their case on black graduate and professional students: most of them attend non-black institutions.[50]

All this does not mean that TBI's no longer have a rationale or a mission. It does suggest, however, that their *raison d'être* might be expressed more effectively in terms of future opportunities rather than past accomplishments.[51] It also suggests that soon rather than later the TBI's must make some painfully frank self-appraisals of their present and prospective enrollment potential, financial status, administration, curricula, and educational quality. And having done so, the TBI's must be prepared to change themselves to meet new conditions.[52]

The academic quality of the TBI's has been the subject of considerable public speculation during the 1960's, and noisy but inconclusive discussions will no doubt continue for some time to come. Perhaps three points need to be understood:

1. There simply is no "scientific," purely objective, or precise procedure for ranking the 2,600 American institutions of higher learning according to quality. There are, however, obvious and demonstrable differences among colleges and universities, and there are many useful measures which may be employed to differentiate among them.

2. It is inaccurate and misleading to consider the 100 TBI's a discrete and homogeneous group, and to compare them with an obviously heterogeneous group of some 2,500 "other" institutions. The TBI's are a

varied group, and they are distributed widely over the spectrum of academic quality. There are some TBI's that are clearly superior to the average "white" college; and assuredly there are scores and maybe hundreds of "white" institutions that are inferior to the average TBI.

3. It nevertheless is true that if the *average* TBI is compared to the *average* of "all other institutions," the former comes out a poor second in most of the conventional academic measures—for example, expenditures per student, faculty salaries, size of library, faculty research and publication, academic credentials of entering freshmen and graduates, and richness and variety in curricular offerings.[53]

The important fact to note, however, is that virtually all of the alleged historical deficiencies of the average TBI result from the long-standing reluctance of the white majority to provide adequate support for black institutions. The federal government, state legislatures, sponsoring church organizations, private agencies, and individual donors all share some degree of responsibility for failing to do enough in years past, when it counted most. Perhaps unwittingly they engaged in self-fulfilling prophecy, for their policies ensured that being black meant being in second place.

The defender of the TBI may indeed feel beleaguered today. He sees little evidence that needed massive support is likely to come from any source. He must be prepared for reductions in enrollment and revenue. He recognizes that a declining proportion of blacks reside in the South, where the TBI's are located. He observes that growing numbers of white institutions lure away many of his best candidates for admission, as well as some of the most competent members of his faculty and administration.[54] Although he probably does not need to be reminded of painful facts, a seemingly endless series of studies and reports confirms the obvious: the TBI's are in trouble, they face new circumstances, they must stop resisting needed reforms, and they must adapt themselves quickly to the new conditions.

If Black Americans and other underrepresented minorities are ever to have proportionate opportunities for access to higher education, there must be concerted and persistent efforts by all types of institutions. The TBI's, however, clearly have an opportunity to play unusual and important roles in preparing black and other youth for a complex, multi-racial, multi-ethnic society. But in order to serve that purpose effectively they must put their own houses in order, consolidate and maximize their scarce resources, and strive for new levels of excellence.

The TBI's remain today among the very few social organizations that Black Americans can call their own. To the Black American searching for pride, identity, and self-confidence in a frequently hostile environment, the TBI assumes an importance quite unrelated to its enrollment statistics, financial status, or presumed rank in the academic procession.[55] The Black American has been accustomed to being outnumbered in America. He knows what it means to be forced to stand at the end of the line. But he intends to change that.

The Black Private Colleges

ALTHOUGH MANY of the 100 TBI's were suffering from enrollment and financial problems in the late 1960's, the situation was most acute at the 51 private senior institutions.[56] Their costs were rising sharply without a corresponding increase in income, and their combined enrollments were actually declining while national black enrollment continued to grow markedly. For years they had been underfinanced and had been forced to struggle to keep their doors open, but by 1970 the prospects seemed particularly grim.[57]

It can be misleading, of course, to generalize about the 51 private senior TBI's. They vary considerably in size, purpose, sponsorship, and financial strength. Least typical of the 51 is Howard University, which enrolls one-sixth of the combined total and is more than three times the size of the next-largest private TBI. Unlike any other black institution, it receives a substantial proportion of its operating revenues directly from federal government appropriations. If Howard is excluded from the list, the remaining group of 50 private senior TBI's enrolled the following numbers of students:

1963	32,301
1968	46,456
1969	45,748
1970	45,358

During the years 1963–68, combined enrollment increased 42.3 per cent—an average annual increase of more than 7 per cent. In 1969, however, enrollment *decreased* by 1.5 per cent, and in 1970 there was a further decline of 0.8 per cent. As the following table indicates, not all of the 50 private TBI's shared in the enrollment decline:

Per cent change	Numbers of institutions experiencing enrollment changes		
	1968–69	1969–70	1968–70
+10.0 or more	7	6	11
+5.0 to +9.9	3	10	4
+0.1 to +4.9	12	9	7
−0.1 to −4.9	10	10	5
−5.0 to −9.9	8	7	9
−10.0 or more	10	8	14
Total	50	50	50

The enrollment increases and decreases at individual institutions between 1968 and 1970 followed no discernible pattern. As the following data show, it was not a case of the large getting larger and the small smaller:

	1968	1970	Change	% change
10 largest in 1968	16,911	16,436	−475	−2.8
30 medium-sized in 1968	25,413	24,599	−814	−3.2
10 smallest in 1968	4,132	4,323	+191	+4.6
Total	46,456	45,348	−1,098	−2.4

Analyses of the ten private TBI's with the largest proportionate increases between 1968 and 1970 and the ten with the greatest losses also reveal no apparent patterns or relationships with geography, academic reputation, initial size, or institutional purpose. What is not known, and hence cannot be assessed, is the extent to which individual institutions grew, remained stable, or declined in enrollment by design. Informal surveys and conversations with many private TBI administrators, however, indicate that virtually all the colleges had room for—and wanted —more students in 1970 than they actually enrolled.[58]

No doubt there were many reasons for the decline in private senior TBI enrollment after 1968, but two factors warrant special mention. First, during the four or five preceding years, federal student-aid programs had been growing rapidly, but after 1968 they tended to level off; without a continuing expansion of such programs, the private TBI's encountered serious difficulty in increasing the number of tuition-paying students. Second, 1968 witnessed a marked acceleration of efforts by non-black colleges to expand their own minority enrollments; it is likely that a substantial number of the most promising black freshmen found more attractive opportunities at, and received larger financial-aid awards from, predominantly white colleges and universities.

Institutional size is an extremely important consideration for the 50 private senior TBI's (again excluding Howard University). Most of them are so small that serious questions may be raised about their ability to provide a curriculum that is both broad and deep at a unit cost within reach of their students and benefactors. The following table shows the range of institutional enrollments in selected years:

Total enrollment	Number of institutions			
	1963	1968	1969	1970
1–499	19	7	7	5
500–749	16	14	18	20
750–999	11	12	7	8
1,000–1,249	2	9	10	8
1,250–1,499	0	5	5	6
1,500 or more	2	3	3	3
	50	50	50	50
Average	653	929	915	907

Higher education specialists in finance and curriculum are not in full agreement about the "optimum," "most efficient," or "most economical" size of four-year colleges, but there are few, if any, who advocate institutional models with fewer than 1,500 full-time students. Obviously, there are a small number of excellent colleges with enrollments of less than 1,500, but invariably these are high-cost institutions that enjoy substantial financial support. The typical private TBI, however, cannot afford the "luxury" of smallness. In 1970, only Howard University (Washington, D.C.), with 9,406 students, plus the three indicated above —Tuskegee Institute (Alabama), Hampton Institute (Virginia), and Bishop College (Texas)—exceeded that minimal figure of 1,500 students.

An obvious course of action for many of the private senior TBI's—and especially the 33 with fewer than 1,000 students each in 1970—would be to enter into mergers and consolidations, thus reducing the total number of institutions but substantially increasing the average size of those remaining, in order to reach some point of curricular and financial efficiency.[59] The following table sets forth two variables—the total combined enrollment of private senior TBI's and the numbers of such institutions—and reveals the impact of one upon the other if "optimum" average institutional size were to be sought through mergers:

Total combined enrollment of all private senior TBI's	Average institutional enrollment if there were the following number of private senior traditionally black institutions			
	51	30	25	20
50,000	980	1,667	2,000	2,500
55,000	1,078	1,833	2,200	2,750
60,000	1,176	2,000	2,400	3,000
65,000	1,275	2,167	2,600	3,250
70,000	1,373	2,333	2,800	3,500
75,000	1,471	2,500	3,000	3,750
80,000	1,569	2,667	3,200	4,000

In the *actual* 1970 situation there were 51 TBI's (including Howard) with a combined enrollment of 54,764, giving an average of 1,074 students. A practical goal, although admittedly difficult to attain, would be an average enrollment of 2,500, with no institution having fewer than 1,500 students. In order to achieve that goal at present total-enrollment levels, there would be need for only about 20 institutions with an average size of 2,500 students. If total private senior TBI enrollment could be increased to nearly 65,000, perhaps 25 institutions would suffice. If the total were 75,000, there could be 30 institutions. To provide *all* of the present 51 senior private TBI's with enough students to attain an average institutional enrollment of 2,500, the total combined student body would have to be 127,500—an increase of 72,736 over the 1970 actual figure of 54,764, or an increase of 133 per cent.

Virtually no TBI's, including the very smallest and those in gravest financial peril, gave clear indication in 1970 that they were prepared to close their doors and merge with neighboring black institutions. Instead, there appeared to be a firm determination to keep *every* TBI open against all odds. The perseverance was commendable, but it may have missed an important point.

The issue probably should not be how many different private senior *institutions* could be kept in operation, but rather how many total *student stations* could be made available and most effectively and efficiently served. The situation in 1970 seemed to suggest that the total enrollment in senior private TBI's could and should be increased substantially. But even if combined enrollment were doubled, there still would be more institutions than needed to do the job.

The question of institutional size is not as critical at the public senior TBI's because they already are larger than the private TBI's and are less dependent upon private funding. The 34 public senior TBI's in 1970 enrolled about 108,000 students, an average of slightly more than 3,000 each. Among the 34, however, there were 12 with enrollments of less than 2,000 each.[60]

No doubt most of the TBI's, both private and public, would serve more students if they had the resources for capital expansion and the financial-aid funds required by severely disadvantaged black students. With few exceptions, the TBI's essentially are residential institutions, so any significant enrollment expansion would require major construction programs. Again with few exceptions, the TBI's serve student bodies that include many youth from low-income families, and it appears unlikely that they will be able to increase their enrollments substantially unless and until there are major new public programs of student support.

3

BARRIERS TO
HIGHER EDUCATION

THE ALLEGED REASONS for minority group underrepresentation in American higher education have been the subject of so much public discussion that further analysis might appear to be unnecessary.[61] In fact, the educational barriers encountered by minority students are more talked about than understood. They are varied, complex, interrelated, reinforcing, and rooted in tradition.[62]

Each of the six conditions discussed below constitutes a barrier only because society explicitly or implicitly wills it.[63] For example, "lack of ability" is not a barrier to entry into the first grade of elementary school, but it is at the point of entry to college. If society were to decide that *everyone* must go to college, just as it decided years ago that all must attend elementary school, the ability barrier would disappear because it would be irrelevant.

The same observation could be made about barriers caused by lack of money. If it were to be decided that all the direct and indirect costs of higher education were to be charged against society at large and that the individual consumer of education would be charged absolutely nothing, the cost barrier would disappear.

The point is that barriers came into being and now continue to operate because society either permitted them to evolve or consciously created them.[64] The following discussion seeks neither to condemn nor to approve of these barriers, nor does it recommend any specific action by society; it merely seeks to point out the nature of certain barriers to higher education and the ways in which American minorities are affected by them.

The Test Barrier

AMERICAN HIGHER EDUCATION was not and is not designed to serve everybody. Despite tremendous enrollment expansion in recent years, barely half of all youth enter higher institutions and an even smaller number complete planned courses of study. Since the system is prepared to handle only half the population, some rationale for exclusion must be established and devices created to make the selection. Historically, two methods have been employed.[65] One permits any high school graduate to begin collegiate study and demonstrate his ability to do the work. The other seeks, through prior selection, to identify those who should be admitted on the basis of their promise. Inevitably, securing access and surviving becomes a competition.

Most of the time, most of society seems to agree to the general proposition that college should be for "the most able." [66] Accordingly, it becomes necessary to apply some test of ability. The process seems simple, but in fact it raises difficult problems. For example, it is not always clear what is meant by "ability." [67] Obviously there are many different kinds of skills and aptitudes, and they may not be equally important or relevant in determining the likelihood of success in higher education. Furthermore, even if the requisite abilities are isolated, labeled, and tested, the testing instrument itself may not actually be measuring the right thing.[68] Finally, there is the stickiest question of all: What is the relative importance of heredity and environment in the shaping of academic aptitude? [69]

Despite the difficulties, there are many instruments that claim to test something or other called ability, intelligence, aptitude, achievement, skill, or attitude. They have become quite common and are now administered at many points in the educational process. Probably the best known are those used to help determine who will and will not be included in the college-bound half of the population. Virtually all of the tests used for college selection have three things in common:

1. They tend to measure verbal ability. This seems reasonable because practically all the learning activity in college depends upon reading, writing, speaking, and listening to standard English with comprehension.

2. The scores they report are relative. This too seems both reasonable and inevitable because there are no known absolutes of ignorance and wisdom, and hence it is logical to rank those who are tested. Thus all scores must be considered and interpreted comparatively, and by definition one-half always are "below average."

3. The abilities and skills they measure are distributed throughout the population according to the familiar symmetrical bell curve. This means that if (a) there is a reasonably varied range of scores or data to be recorded and (b) a fairly large number of cases are

measured, then most scores are clustered near the average and rapidly decrease in number as they move away from the average.

Any normal distribution (i.e., bell curve) has certain unfailing and predictable statistical characteristics that apply no matter what it is that is being measured. One of these characteristics, of course, is that scores are spread around a central point or average. The statistic usually employed to describe the amount of spread is called the standard deviation (S.D.).[70] In effect, it describes accurately and precisely how many cases actually fall within specified segments of a bell curve. By definition, it always works out as follows:

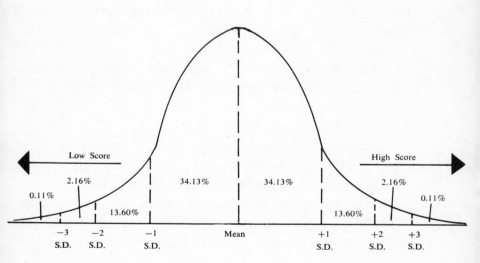

The designations on the horizontal base line represent standard deviations. The percentages indicate the proportion of cases falling between the dotted lines. To illustrate, in this and in all normal distributions, 34.13 per cent of all cases fall between the mean and $+1$ standard deviation. Or, no more than 2.27 per cent of all cases ever exceed two standard deviations above the mean. The nature of normal distribution and the significance of a standard deviation must be appreciated in order to understand the impact of test scores on minority access to higher education.

The crucial fact is this: Virtually every test that purports to measure educational aptitude or achievement reveals that the mean of the scores of minority youth is about one standard deviation below the mean of the scores of the rest of the population. This disturbing observation has been examined and re-examined in test after test, and it appears to be consistent.[71]

The simplest way to demonstrate the impact of this statistical fact is to provide a hypothetical example. If 10,000 representative eighteen-year-old Americans were tested, at least 1,500 (i.e., 15 per cent) of them would be members of the four minority groups discussed in this report, and 8,500 would be "all others." Assuming a normal distribution of scores and the typical one standard-deviation difference between the means of the minority students and "all others," the 10,000 scores would be distributed as follows:

Score range	"All others"	Minority students	Total
Absolute maximum			
+3 S.D.	9	2 ⎫	9
+2 S.D.	184	⎬ 2	186
+1 S.D.	1,156	32	1,188
Mean	2,901	204	3,105
	2,901	512	3,413
−1 S.D.		(minority mean)	
−2 S.D.	1,156	512	1,668
−3 S.D.	184	204	388
Absolute minimum	9	34	43

This chart is a simple example of the typical fashion in which scores are distributed whenever verbal-ability tests are given to large representative groups of students.

The reasons for the consistent phenomenon of low minority scores prompt much speculation, but the only point to be made here is this: Test scores, if used *without* discrimination and *without* reference to sub-groups within the total population, constitute a major barrier for minority youth seeking access to higher education. To illustrate, if the distribution example shown above were to be used strictly and arbitrarily it would yield these results:

1. If a moderately selective university were to take all of its students from approximately the top one-sixth of the ability spectrum, its "talent pool" would include

only 2.5 per cent (34 out of 1,383) from the minority groups.[72]

2. If American higher institutions collectively were to enroll everybody scoring above the arithmetic mean of "all others," only 5.3 per cent (238 out of 4,488) of that pool would come from the minority groups. Expressed another way, higher education would be serving 50 per cent of "all others" but only 15.9 per cent of all the minority youth.

3. Even if American higher institutions collectively were to enroll everybody scoring above the mean of the *minority* groups, only 9.5 per cent (750 out of 7,901) of that pool would come from the minority groups. Expressed another way, in order to serve 50 per cent of all minority youth, higher education would be obliged to enroll 84.1 per cent of "all others."

All of the foregoing underscores the difficulty of achieving equitable representation for minorities in higher education if any of the conventional rank-ordered tests of academic ability are employed impartially, literally, and automatically to determine admissibility. Of course, no admissions officer anywhere would use test scores in such a thoughtless fashion. But as long as the mean score for minority youth is one standard deviation below the mean of "all others," a massive problem remains.[73]

This frustrating situation has invited public discussion and stimulated persistent attacks on testing.[74] Serious and appropriate questions are repeatedly raised about (*a*) the reasons minority youth do not score well, (*b*) the alleged "cultural bias" of many tests, (*c*) the predictive value of tests,[75] and (*d*) the possibility that tests do not actually measure appropriate abilities. But despite the attacks on standardized tests, no generally accepted alternative devices for selection have been developed.

Critics of educational testing sometimes generalize from exceptions and cite "low scorers" who attained scholastic eminence. In fact, general-ability test scores merely indicate probabilities based on empirical evidence, and testers' evaluations and predictions for population groups (rather than for individual persons) within measured ability ranges are remarkably on target. Psychometricians point out that their tests are no more responsible for inequitable distribution of academic skills than is the thermometer responsible for fluctuations in temperature. They both just measure what is, but they don't create it. Nevertheless, the criticism continues, and testers are blamed for the bad news they report.

Actually, the arguments go full circle. If society is only going to enroll half its youth in higher education, some exclusionary device inevitably must be employed. Even if it is to be "first come—first served," half will arrive at the gate after it is closed, and the tardy ones probably will find some basis for questioning the fairness of the procedure.

Perhaps the most important question about present educational-testing techniques is this: Do they discriminate against minority youth *as* minority youth and *because* they are minority youth? Despite prolonged and often bitter debate, it does not appear that a provable affirmative answer is forthcoming. But the fact remains: conventional tests of conventional academic ability reveal that minority youth do not score well, and hence they encounter difficulty in getting into college.

The Barrier of Poor Preparation

VIRTUALLY all tests for college entry seek to measure academic aptitudes and skills which presumably were developed over many years. It logically follows, therefore, that the quality and style of an individual's prior environment inevitably will affect his performance on standardized national tests.[76] Since formal education is an important segment of life for most of the individual's first eighteen years, and since school activities and demands closely resemble those of college,[77] the quality, nature, and extent of prior schooling are major factors in determining who is likely to go to and succeed in college.[78] The point is so obvious and has been reported so widely that it requires little elaboration here. It may simply be noted that minority-group students

do not complete high school in as large numbers, proportionately, as do "all others" [79]

tend, in proportionately larger numbers than "all others," to elect or to be counseled into taking non-academic, vocational, and technical programs in high school more often than not live in communities that have primary and secondary schools with facilities, faculties, libraries, and cultural resources below the national average [80]

usually attend schools in which they are effectively segregated from the majority students with whom they later must compete for college entry.[81]

The Money Barrier

AMERICAN HIGHER education is a large, complex, and costly industry which secures its income from public tax revenues, tax-deductible gifts, and individual students and their families. Expenditures and costs per student for higher education vary considerably across the country and according to the type and purpose of institution. Two different sets of figures often are cited: one is the per capita expenditure by an institution, and the other is the cost incurred by a student attending that institution. The latter usually is expressed as a typical annual-expense budget for a resident or non-resident student, and includes provision for tuition, fees, room and board (or lunches and local carfare), books, and some personal incidentals. In 1970–71 the average annual-expense budget for undergraduate resident students was about $4,000 at private and $2,000 at public institutions. It ranged from as low as $1,000 at some public, non-resident, community colleges in urban centers to nearly $5,000 at a few prestigious private universities in the Northeast.[82]

The costs for the individual and his family obviously

64

are sufficiently high to make it virtually impossible for substantial proportions of the population even to consider higher education unless gifts, scholarships, and other forms of aid reduce the personal bill. This cost barrier particularly hurts America's racial and ethnic minorities because their family incomes are well below national averages. For example, the Census Bureau reported the following data about the distribution of families by income in 1968:[83]

	White	Non-white
Under $5,000	20%	45%
$5,000–$9,999	38	35
$10,000–$14,999	26	15
$15,000 and over	16	5
	100%	100%

The median family income in 1968 for whites was $8,937; for non-whites it was only $5,590, or 63 per cent of the figure for whites.

Since college costs are high and still rising, and since there is considerable variation in family income, it is not surprising to discover that higher education enrollment is skewed. About half of all current students come from families in the top economic quarter; barely 6 or 8 per cent come from families in the lowest quarter.[84] Since minority families are clustered disproportionately at the lower end of the economic bell curve, the collegiate enrollment of their children is predictably low.[85]

Unless and until American society decides to assume total public financial responsibility for higher education, it seems clear that enrollment will continue to be determined in large measure by parental resources. Unless and until minority groups attain income levels comparable to that of the white majority, it seems clear that the economic barrier to higher education will be forbidding to most minority youth.[86]

The Distance Barrier

MANY STUDIES in recent years have documented a fact that appears disarmingly obvious at first reading: When American higher institutions are made more readily accessible geographically, financially, and academically, their enrollments go up.[87] This seems to confirm the claim that expanded educational supply has not yet exceeded individual demand—assuming, of course, that the price and other considerations are right.

Some institutions have increased enrollment by lowering prices (normally by changing from private to public sponsorship), by dropping entrance requirements, or by moving facilities closer to population centers.[88] Changes of these types are particularly important to minority groups because institutional inaccessibility is one of the major frustrations they face. The financial and test barriers were discussed above; now a word about the distance barrier is in order.

The great majority of American college students attend institutions relatively close to home. As a general rule, the less wealthy the student, the closer he stays to

68   MINORITY ACCESS TO COLLEGE

home. It obviously follows, therefore, that distance from residence to some higher education facility helps to determine the probability of enrollment. Since an ever-growing number of minority youth live in the central cities of major metropolitan areas, the availability there of low-cost, open-door, easily reached colleges and universities is extremely important.[89] Even an additional bus or subway ride makes a difference and depresses minority enrollment.

The extent to which minority populations have grown in urban centers is remarkable. Census data about America's thirty largest cities reveal that between 1950 and 1967 the proportion of the black population increased substantially.[90] The following table provides detailed information:

PERCENTAGE OF BLACKS IN EACH OF
THE THIRTY LARGEST U.S. CITIES *

			1950	1960	1967 (est.)
1.	Washington, D.C.	(9)	35%	54%	69%
2.	Newark	(30)	17	34	49
3.	Atlanta	(24)	37	38	44
4.	Baltimore	(6)	24	35	41
5.	New Orleans	(15)	32	37	41
6.	Memphis	(22)	37	37	40
7.	Detroit	(5)	16	29	39
8.	St. Louis	(10)	18	29	37
9.	Cleveland	(8)	16	29	34
10.	Philadelphia	(4)	18	26	33

11. Chicago	(2)	14	23	30
12. Cincinnati	(21)	16	22	24
13. Indianapolis	(26)	15	21	24
14. Houston	(7)	21	23	22
15. Dallas	(14)	13	19	22
16. Kansas City, Mo.	(27)	12	18	22
17. Pittsburgh	(16)	12	17	21
18. New York	(1)	10	14	19
19. Columbus	(28)	12	16	19
20. Los Angeles	(3)	9	14	18
21. Buffalo	(20)	6	13	17
22. Boston	(13)	5	9	15
23. Milwaukee	(11)	3	8	14
24. San Francisco	(12)	6	10	14
25. Denver	(23)	4	6	9
26. San Antonio	(17)	7	7	8
27. San Diego	(18)	5	6	7
28. Seattle	(19)	3	5	7
29. Phoenix	(29)	5	5	5
30. Minneapolis	(25)	1	2	4

* The cities are ranked according to the percentage of blacks in 1967. The number in parentheses after the name of the city is its rank in total population.

As the data clearly show, significant changes have taken place in the country's ten largest metropolitan centers. In Washington, D.C., America's "blackest" major city, the Negro percentage increased from 35 to 69 between 1950 and 1967.[91] In Baltimore, it rose from 24 to 41; in Detroit, 16 to 39; in St. Louis, 18 to 37; in Cleveland, 16 to 34; in Philadelphia, 18 to 33; in Chicago, 14 to 30;[92] in New York, 10 to 19;[93] and in Los Angeles, 9 to 18. Houston showed little change (21 to 22), but that was due to the fact that the space industry has attracted so many whites to that city.

Comparable information about Mexican Americans, Puerto Ricans, and American Indians is not readily available, but it is certain that they too have become more urbanized and now constitute sizable proportions of city populations. For example, Los Angeles probably has more Mexican Americans than Black Americans, and New York's Puerto Rican population is approaching the size of the local black community. The impact on elementary and secondary schooling and on access to higher education is obvious.[94]

Almost every large American urban center has a collection of educational institutions that includes the following: a major private university; a large public university; a collection of small, church-related, liberal arts colleges; and a public, two-year community college. The last-named is likely to be less than ten years old, to be the most rapidly growing (and perhaps already the largest) institution in the area, and to enroll more minority students than all the other neighboring colleges and universities combined.

The increase in institutional accessibility represented by the opening of new urban community colleges is probably the single most important reason for the increase in minority enrollment during the 1960's.[95] These institutions are now serving almost one-third of the total national black enrollment (and, incidentally, almost as many as all the traditionally black colleges combined), and they attracted about half of all new black freshmen in 1970.

If the underrepresentation of American minorities in higher education is to be reduced significantly within the next decade, it seems clear that most of the expansion of freshman minority enrollment will continue to take place in

the public rather than the private sector

areas other than the South

low-cost rather than high-cost institutions

colleges located in central cities rather than in suburbs or rural areas

colleges other than traditionally black institutions.

The public two-year college appears to best fit the need. But as it succeeds in serving more minority youth, a new problem is likely to emerge: Will minority students be enabled to continue in *higher* higher education?

The Motivation Barrier

DESPITE THE SOCIAL and economic pressures upon all young Americans to continue education beyond high school, the fact remains that college attendance is not prescribed by law, and every student goes by choice. Not all of the ablest, the wealthiest, or those living across the street from a campus choose to go to college. And obviously some others with less impressive academic credentials and bank accounts do choose to go, are admitted, and do succeed. The difference presumably is motivation— an ill-defined but crucial mixture of personal ambition, drive, determination, and persistence.[96]

The importance of motivation in determining the likelihood of admission to college varies in relation to the other factors described above. The less the "native ability," the longer and more assiduously the student must study. The smaller the family financial resources, the harder the student must work, save, and sacrifice. The poorer the quality of the high school from which he comes, the more the student must seek extramural aid, inspiration, and cultural stimulation. Sufficient individual determination and diligence in the face of long odds often lead to results that defy the best-programmed computerized prognostications.[97]

It is alleged by many laymen and some educators that minority students, as a group, are not sufficiently motivated to prepare for, and do the work required in, college.[98] Presumably if they would just study longer, work harder, and save more, they too could overcome the handicaps encountered and conquered by the disadvantaged of previous generations. There is, of course, no way to prove or disprove this thesis, and hence it is impossible to determine whether, in fact, lack of motivation is a barrier for minority youth.[99]

Others would argue, perhaps correctly, that the growing (although still underrepresented) minority enrollment is compelling testimony to the strong motivation of this generation's severely disadvantaged youth. The extraordinary fact is that there are so many, rather than so few, minority college students who seem to belie social, economic, and academic expectations.[100]

The Racial Barrier

UNTIL RECENTLY, most writers simply failed to mention or discuss the impact of American racism on the educational system.[101] There is clear evidence that racist practices, carried out through centuries of American history, are responsible for virtually all the barriers to higher education that have been described above.[102] Continued and persistent exploitation, deprivation, segregation, and denial of opportunity have exacted a fearful but predictable toll.[103] Now, of course, even if a completely race-free, color-blind, unprejudiced policy of full and equal opportunity for all were to be proclaimed and implemented, it would tend over the short term to perpetuate rather than remove present inequities.[104]

Today virtually no candidate is denied admission to any American college or university *because* he is black, Indian, Puerto Rican, or Mexican American. Indeed, at many institutions he may appear to receive preferential treatment. But in fact he suffers a serious competitive disability.[105] The minority student approaches the narrow

74

college gate with the heavy burdens of inadequate prior
schooling, lower test scores, and smaller income. Those burdens were placed on his back by a social system that classified people and determined their worth according to skin
color.[106]

4
EFFORTS TO LOWER
THE BARRIERS

ON THURSDAY, April 4, 1968, in Memphis, Tennessee, Martin Luther King, Jr., was assassinated. That tragic event precipitated a crisis in relations between America's white and black populations. Tensions had been growing for years, of course, and increasing racial polarization and violence caused widespread fear after the murder that American society would tear itself apart.

Riots had been making headlines for some time. In 1963 there were serious disorders in Birmingham, Savannah, Cambridge (Md.), Chicago, and Philadelphia. In 1964 there were disruptions in Jacksonville, Cleveland, St. Augustine, Philadelphia (Miss.), New York, Rochester, Jersey City, and the Chicago suburb of Dixmoor. In 1965 there were riots in Bogalusa (La.) and a massive upheaval in the Watts area of Los Angeles. The pattern continued in 1966, with new disorders in Watts, Chicago, Cleveland, and Baltimore. In 1967 the situation became even more acute, and serious disorders broke out in Nashville, Houston, Tampa, Cincinnati, Atlanta, Newark, Detroit, and Plainfield and New Brunswick (N.J.).[107] After five consecutive "long hot summers," it is small wonder that the murder of Dr. King and its riotous aftermath in the spring of 1968 stirred fearful white America to action. The non-Negro colleges had not been completely idle during the years preceding the King assassination. Many white professors and college students had been deeply troubled by continuing evidence of racism in American society, and in a variety of ways they tried to help improve conditions. Volunteers "went South" to work in voter-registration drives, teach in Negro colleges, and participate in civil rights sit-ins and demonstrations. Others served as tutors for ghetto youngsters. Some, armed with brooms and paint brushes, set out to clean up slums. But few of these activities significantly affected many of the white campuses themselves.

Minority enrollments at some of the non-black colleges had been increasing sharply throughout the 1960's, but the numbers and proportions generally remained small.[108] In any event, there had been little fanfare, and few people were aware that changes were taking place. The King murder, however, awakened the consciences of many whites who previously had been untouched by "the racial issue." It led to their realization that institutions of higher learning were de facto segregated, and it stimulated a flurry of activity that has not yet subsided. The obvious and immediate task in 1968 was to find ways of lowering the barriers that were limiting minority access to higher education. It was easier said than done.

Reaching Out to a New Population

MOST OF THE historically non-black colleges discovered very quickly that they had virtually no contacts with the sources of supply of minority students. Their recruitment programs tended to focus on the better private and public secondary schools in high-income areas, and few of those high schools enrolled very many minority youth. For years, white college-admissions officers had cultivated guidance counselors at the "right" schools, but they had generally ignored Southern black and urban ghetto secondary institutions because these had so few graduates who could both qualify academically and satisfy the bursar's demands.[109] Guidance counselors, even at the stronger high schools, rarely took the initiative to recommend minority youth, because it seemed a futile exercise which would only raise hopes and then dash them.

Many colleges tried new approaches in 1968.[110] They began to visit high schools in poor neighborhoods. There they discovered that white recruiters often encountered black skepticism, and so they began to add minority people to their admissions staffs. They learned that some of their own few black enrollees wanted to help recruit, and that such students could best persuade doubting high school pupils of the colleges' sincerity and hospitality. They also discovered that blacks were not the only underrepresented minority, and they began to seek out Mexican American and Puerto Rican candidates.

The colleges also became aware that the normal guidance and counseling procedures in many of the ghetto schools simply were not functioning for minority students. So college recruiters turned to extramural agencies—civil rights organizations, churches, and community-action groups—for help in identifying promising diamonds in the rough.

Support for scores of college-recruitment programs was provided by philanthropic organizations and interested individuals.[111] Many academic institutions, without fanfare or external financial support, reordered their own priorities and used their own funds to seek more minority students. Invariably, the recruitment efforts cost more in money and man-hours than the colleges had anticipated. Once they were started, however, it became virtually impossible to discontinue them, even had the colleges wished to do so. Higher education appeared to have embarked on a strange new adventure, for now some institutions were assiduously pursuing the very students who would have been rejected out of hand the year before.

It is difficult to determine how effective the ambitious minority-recruitment programs have been. At least three phenomena appear to be worth noting:

1. Most of the best-publicized efforts probably reshuffled rather than increased the total minority enrollment. Practically all the new students enrolled in prestigious white institutions would have attended traditionally black or less demanding and less attractive white colleges. No doubt the "creaming" process caused a chain reaction and created some openings farther back in the academic procession, but many of the less-favored institutions, black and white, felt that they were being raided by recent converts to the cause of racial justice and that some minority students were being exploited to assuage white guilt at wealthy institutions.

2. Some of the universities appeared to be engaged in "collegiate bussing." Many white colleges from all over the country concentrated their efforts on the deep South and on such obvious but usually distant ghettos as Harlem, Bedford-Stuyvesant, Cleveland's Hough, and Watts. Recruiters practically stumbled over each other in the well-known, high-density black areas, but too often they ignored their own local black communities.

3. There was an understandable tendency for colleges to look for dark-skinned candidates who had all the characteristics of their usual crop of white applicants. Accordingly, recruitment efforts became talent searches based on the assumption that "somewhere out there" a substantial supply of poor but bright and deserving minority youth were awaiting discovery. It was learned quickly that the number of conventionally qualified and high-scoring minority students was small and that increased minority enrollment could be achieved only by reaching much deeper into the conventionally measured ability pool.[112]

Bending Admissions Standards

DETERMINING admissibility has always been more an art than a science, and even the most selective colleges always have taken "high-risk" students. For decades, institutions quietly found good and sufficient reasons to admit candidates who were blessed with extraordinary athletic ability or influential family connections, but who had academic credentials far below "normal" for entering freshmen. Indeed, almost by definition the bottom tenth, quarter, third, or half of the entering group at most colleges consists of academic starters who are doubtful finishers.

But when growing numbers of fairly selective, non-black institutions began to increase their minority enrollments by bending traditional admissions requirements and standards, public attention was attracted to "high-risk" students.[113] In large measure, the colleges themselves were responsible for the publicity. They had three good reasons for telling their story: They hoped to protect institutional reputations for excellence by stressing the fact that poorly prepared minority students really were "exceptions"; they

84

needed to make some explanation to better-qualified, non-minority candidates who had been denied admission and who were convinced that they were the victims of reverse discrimination; finally, it provided an opportunity for the colleges to proclaim their own virtue.

There were other more significant results of the new "high-risk" admissions practices. For example, some institutions now began to look seriously and questioningly at long-established admissions procedures, and greater flexibility was encouraged. Certain specified high school course requirements were dropped, admission test scores were interpreted less rigidly, and there was increased concern about so-called non-intellective factors that might be useful in predicting college success. All these issues had been the subject of polite discussion within the professional educational fraternity for years, but now the debate was public, and changes actually were occurring.[114]

By no means was or is there unanimous support for alleged tinkering with college admissions standards. Some alumni fear that their degrees will now be devalued. Some faculty members complain that they should not be expected to waste their time on the unprepared. Some college presidents worry about the impact of adverse publicity on conservative state legislators and potential benefactors. The arguments spilled out of campuses, received media amplification, entered the political arena, and attracted comment from high places, including the Office of the Vice-President of the United States.[115]

Almost without exception, college and university announcements of "high-risk programs" and "special exceptions to regular admission standards" were accompanied by statements declaring that internal academic standards and degree requirements would remain unchanged. In other words, it would be easier for minority students to get in— but as difficult as ever to stay in and earn degrees.

Information about the academic survival of recently admitted "high-risk" minority students is so incomplete that it is impossible to make precise analyses of their performances. It appears likely, however, that the attrition was lower than the academic credentials and entrance test scores of the students would have led one to predict. It is not certain at this juncture to what degree the apparent success was the result of intensive remedial courses, better-than-expected student performance and persistence, or compassionate grading practices.

The last-named consideration is particularly difficult to assess. The typical standardized admissions test is administered to a large number of students under identical and controlled conditions; it is scored mechanically and impersonally; and the results obtained by students are distributed on a normal bell curve. On the other hand, professors' grades are determined individually (and to a degree subjectively) under widely varying conditions, are rarely subject to review by other parties, and are not necessarily rank-ordered or "bell curved."

This is not to suggest that one system is better or more accurate than the other, but rather that they obviously are different. The admissions tests are designed to predict how students are likely to perform in college, but the accuracy of those predictions depends in large measure upon consistency, objectivity, and integrity on the part of faculty members. If the latter, consciously or unconsciously, permit their own sentiments unduly to influence their evaluations of student performance, they may be engaged in self-fulfilling prophecy and hence reducing the predictive value of admissions tests.

Measuring the success or failure of "not normally admissible" minority students is complicated further by substantial differences in institutional standards and expectations. Hence, it is important to determine if an individual is labeled "high-risk" because of his rank within his own college class or his rank among *all* freshmen at *all* higher institutions. A "high-risk" student at an Ivy League university, for example, may enter with credentials far below those of the average of his classmates, but nevertheless be in the top five per cent of all American youth and the top one per cent of minority youth. His subsequent academic success should raise few eyebrows.

But the Ivy League is atypical. At hundreds of less selective, less prestigious, and less demanding colleges and universities, a large number of truly "high-risk" students also appear to have been successful. Too often, however, it is forgotten that they were accepted by admissions officers who were trying "to beat the odds." A simple illustration makes the point: Assume that prior experience revealed that nine out of ten students with certain entrance scores normally failed to survive the academic competition at a particular college. Knowing this, the admissions officer —relying on his intuition and other considerations—sought to identify the *one* in ten who was most likely to succeed and be the exception to the rule. Statistically, that *one* was a "high-risk," but if he survived it did not mean that the test was "wrong" in its prediction of likely failure. It probably meant that the admissions officer performed his art skillfully and guessed correctly.

Finally, the very act of admitting a "high-risk" minority student to college may affect his own attitudes and motivation, and hence may confound some earlier pessimistic predictions about his academic performance. If he knows that he is starting with competitive disadvantages, but that someone is betting on him, he may be prompted to work harder and rise to the challenge. On the other hand, of course, he may be one of those who crack and fail all the sooner because they set unrealistic goals for themselves.

In summary, then, there is considerable evidence that since 1968 there has been an effective lowering of the test barrier for substantial numbers of minority students. Generally, this has been achieved not by abolishing or significantly altering the tests themselves, but rather by interpreting test scores in a new light and recognizing the limitations of present devices for measurement, prediction, and academic evaluation.[116] It still is too early to tell if this extension of college opportunity to formerly inadmissible minority students will (*a*) reveal a hitherto unidentified talent pool, (*b*) materially change the academic and degree standards of institutions, or (c) merely delay the conventional sorting and rank-ordering of people by moving it from post-high school to post-college. No doubt these issues will be grist for the research mills for years to come.

Paying the Bill

ONE OF THE MOST difficult barriers to remove has been cost. In recent years the major source of student financial aid has been the federal government, but all of its programs of direct grants, guaranteed loans, and payment for campus jobs have failed to meet the growing demands during a period of rapidly rising educational costs.[117]

Immediately after the King assassination there was an increase in private giving earmarked to enable higher institutions to help minority students, but that quickly slowed to a trickle. Almost from the beginning of the concerted drive to enroll more minority students, the major philanthropies and foundations realized that the nationwide needs of minority undergraduates far exceeded their resources, and they reluctantly concluded that they could only deal with limited programmatic aspects of the minority-student problem.[118]

The colleges themselves were caught in the middle. They alone were the purveyors of educational services; there was a growing demand for those services by people who couldn't pay for them; and the colleges could hardly afford

90

to give them away. All higher institutions—and especially those in the private sector—quickly discovered four things:

1. The proportion of minority students who came from low-income and impoverished families was larger than they had expected. The colleges had been accustomed to working out financial-aid packages for lower-middle-class white students, but the new and very poor minority students had needs that were both greater *and* different. For example, minority students often arrived on campus without adequate wardrobes, books, supplies, money for essential personal expenses, or needed items for partially furnished dormitory rooms. The typical financial-aid awards required by poor minority youth turned out to be much larger than had been anticipated.

2. Each college's total financial-aid budget seemed to grow at a geometric rate. In the emotion-charged days after Dr. King's death, many institutions announced plans to admit and provide support for modest numbers of poor minority students. Each successive year they were faced with demands to admit even more, and meanwhile, of course, they had continuing responsibility for the scholarship students already enrolled. All these factors, plus rapidly rising general expenses, created unanticipated budgetary squeezes.

3. Colleges discovered that mushrooming financial-aid budgets represented only a portion of the true cost of trying to serve underprepared minority students. Additional personal and academic counseling was often required and had to be paid for. Special extracurricular programs and facilities sometimes were provided at extra cost. High-cost remedial programs had to be instituted.

Indeed, at some unfortunate campuses there was the added expense of repairing buildings and grounds damaged during disruptions and riots which had racial overtones.

4. Analyses of the higher-than-expected financial-aid costs revealed, to the concern of many college administrators, that the increased enrollment of low-income minority students was at the expense of middle-income (and presumably white) students who normally needed at least some of the scholarship support which was now in short supply. At many private institutions it was discovered, for example, that 8 or 10 per cent of the entering class might consist of minority students but that they were receiving anywhere from 35 to 50 per cent of all the financial-aid funds available for freshmen. Some university administrators feared that the student body soon would consist only of the very rich and the very poor, and that one form of underrepresentation was merely being replaced by another.

All the evidence seemed to confirm the obvious: minority enrollments simply could not increase to the point of parity unless and until massive funds for student support were made available. The sums needed nationally clearly would exceed a billion dollars annually, and nothing short of a major change in federal funding policies for higher education could provide resources of such magnitude. Ultimately, such a decision would have to be made in the polling booth by citizens prepared to tax themselves for that purpose.

Changing the Students

IN A NUMBER OF respects, some subtle and some obvious, the historically white, middle-class colleges and the new (and usually low-income) minority students simply were different. Each tried to change the other. Results have been mixed, and it is difficult at this point to determine who was the more successful. It is likely, however, that neither will be quite the same.

Many colleges set up pre-freshman summer programs for incoming minority students. These usually featured remedial courses in basic language and mathematical skills, but perhaps more important were the incidental efforts to help the new students to "adjust" to the social and intellectual life of the institution and to learn the rules of the campus game.

Virtually all institutions expanded their orientation activities in recognition of "the special needs" of their new minority clientele. The colleges sometimes missed the target and made the minority students feel more like guests than members of the family.

Many underprepared minority students were required to

take special remedial courses without full college credit. Formal and informal tutoring arrangements were set up. Reduced course loads were prescribed for some students. The justification for all these adjustments in the "normal" educational program was both obvious and reasonable: they were designed to help the minority student catch up to, and become more like, the regular student.[119]

At this juncture, it is impossible to determine whether or not these efforts are achieving their objectives. Virtually every college and university has its own well-publicized success story, but apparently few thought it prudent to list those students who fell by the wayside. Many evaluative reports were issued, but ordinarily they were produced by the same college administrators responsible for the special minority programs. The reports may have been self-serving and more optimistic than warranted by the facts.

Nevertheless, it clearly is true that scores, hundreds, or perhaps thousands of minority youth since 1968 received unanticipated opportunities to attend college, were profoundly affected and stimulated by the experience, and performed with unexpected academic distinction. We may never really know the ratio of failures to successes. But even one success is more than none.

Changing the Institutions

THE LATTER YEARS of the 1960's were turbulent ones for American higher education.[120] Basic questions were raised about institutional purposes and procedures, and many once-sacred cows were dragged to the slaughterhouse. Rioting, violence, and disruption were limited to about one-quarter of America's 2,600 colleges and universities, but the impact was felt on every campus and throughout the population at large. The causes of widespread campus unrest were and are varied and complex, and they will be probed and analyzed for years to come. Clearly, a prime cause has been youthful dissatisfaction with a society allegedly suffering from maldistributed opportunity and affluence.[121]

It seems fair to observe that the increased minority enrollment was more a response to, than a cause of, persistent pressures for campus changes. Unfortunately, however, the presence of a new, visible, and different group on campus during a period of turmoil made it vulnerable to simplistic charges that somehow it was responsible for the end of academic tranquillity.[122] Such allegations usually

95

were unfounded. In fact, most new minority enrollees at white colleges seemed more intent on getting into "the system" than on destroying it.

This is not to say that expanded minority enrollment on white campuses left the colleges and universities unchanged.[123] Quite the contrary. It was pointed out above that the entire admissions process was re-examined and modified, and the pattern of freshman studies suddenly became surprisingly flexible. Other changes also came about, and no doubt more are in the offing. The following are examples:

   colleges began intensive searches for minority-group faculty members, administrators, and trustees

   "relevance" became a cliché, and colleges increasingly became involved with neighboring, non-campus minority people and problems

   courses of study, syllabi, and the curriculum at large were re-examined, found to be wanting, and altered with an infusion of "ethnic studies" [124]

   distributional requirements for the degree were made more flexible, and even teaching styles were modified to some extent

   periods of academic probation were extended to give underprepared minority students more time to "catch up"

   grading procedures were changed and in some cases abandoned for pass-fail arrangements; conventional competitive practices were de-emphasized.

5
CONCLUSIONS AND PROJECTIONS

DESPITE IMPRESSIVE GAINS in the 1960's, even greater efforts will be required in the future to remove the barriers that restrict the entry of Black American, Mexican American, Puerto Rican, and American Indian youth into higher education. By no means are all Americans agreed that such a goal is desirable or attainable.

There are many sincere but troubled people who object to persistent efforts by social scientists and educators to classify, count, sort, test, and measure individuals, and to place them in pigeonholes according to race, ethnic group, religion, occupation, income, intelligence, and dozens of other criteria. It is alleged that such data exaggerate differences, raise expectations, create tensions, and exacerbate rather than solve social problems. Perhaps so. Nevertheless, social statistics *do* exist and individuals *do* identify themselves with social sub-groups. A return to some simpler age of statistical ignorance may be appealing, but it is virtually impossible. Furthermore, racial data will continue

99

to be necessary for as long as racial inequities persist. How else can society measure its progress toward justice?

There is temptation to be melodramatic about the problems of minority education. The substantial extension of higher education opportunities for underrepresented minorities could indeed lead to profound social adjustments, and hence it is threatening to some people.[125] The lowering of barriers that now restrict certain groups might very well result in universal higher education, which in turn might upset the "social ecology" and lead to far-reaching changes in social expectation, organization, and behavior.[126] The stakes appear to be large.

And yet the present situation is neither strange nor new. From its earliest days, America has been engaged in a continuing struggle between those seeking to extend or to restrict opportunity for the latest claimants to equality.

The Record Seems to Show . . .

IT IS IMPOSSIBLE to report any definitive conclusions, because conditions affecting minority access to higher education are changing rapidly. Most of the efforts to increase minority opportunities were started recently and are still in progress. Nevertheless, the following tentative observations may be reported.

The number of conventionally "qualified" minority eighteen-year-olds is probably much smaller than had been expected and hoped by minority spokesmen.[127] Direct responsibility for increasing that number falls more heavily on elementary and secondary schools than on higher institutions. However, colleges and universities are responsible for the staffing of lower schools and for helping to determine their educational priorities.

Institutions of higher education and our society in general have not organized themselves effectively to handle large enrollment increases of minority youth. State planning is lagging.[128] State legislatures pinch budgets. Major federal support has not materialized. Most institutions, private and public, black and white, have tended merely to

101

react to minority pressures rather than to take the initiative in planning. Most institutions simply have no long-term policy respecting minority enrollment.

Some three or four dozen public and private, predominantly white institutions in positions of leadership have made commitments to increase minority enrollment substantially. This usually means that they are prepared to have a freshman class that includes 10 per cent or more minority students. There are no signs that large numbers of other institutions either desire or are able to follow their lead.

Some highly selective, competitive, and prestigious colleges and universities have bent admissions and performance standards and they have survived. Less selective institutions have less to bend, and they are less inclined to be willing to bend. The more secure an institution's reputation, the more likely it is to be able and willing to adapt itself to a new population.

Minority enrollment has both increased and shifted during the last decade. The shifts (from traditionally black institutions, and especially to the prestigious, private, nonblack, senior colleges) have attracted more attention than the great numerical increases (in public, urban, and community colleges).

The shortage of funds for student support is the major factor now holding down minority enrollment. Minority programs at some of the leading colleges and universities are in jeopardy, and recent growth in minority enrollment at private institutions may ease off. It is almost universally assumed that only the federal government is capable of dealing with the financial-aid problem. It is almost universally feared that the needed aid will not be forthcoming in the near future.

Institutions of higher learning have not worked together effectively to use their limited resources more efficiently or to address themselves cooperatively to the problems of local minority populations. Colleges and universities consistently have maintained a jealous independence and have refused to permit consortia to be successful. As a result, clusters of urban institutions have failed to maximize opportunities for minorities.

High school guidance programs, North and South, are middle-class oriented and are markedly inadequate as far as minority youth and the poor are concerned. Unless and until secondary school personnel and practices are changed, minority students will continue to be dependent upon out-of-school agencies and advocates.

Despite glowing and over-publicized stories about exceptions to the rule, "high-risk" students indeed are academic risks and do require special handling and assistance. If colleges and universities do not recognize this fact, they (and their easily disenchanted new clientele) must be prepared to accept very high academic attrition and further estrangement from the minority communities.

The needs and demands of minority students are forcing many colleges and universities to re-examine and re-define their responsibilities for remediation, skill-training, and general education. There are some signs that at the undergraduate level there is growing faculty recognition of the need to teach the student as well as the subject.

Most remedial and compensatory efforts for minority (and for all other) youth have failed to meet their goals. Perhaps the goals were set too high. Perhaps the programs were poorly designed or poorly executed. Perhaps it is impossible to repair sixteen years of disability in sixteen weeks. Data indicate that the effectiveness of remediation declines sharply as the age of the student increases.

The supply of factual information required for serious analysis of minority education problems is growing rapidly, but nevertheless most data continue to be sketchy, incomplete, tentative, and of questionable objectivity.

From This Point On . . .

THE HIGHER EDUCATION scene in America has changed so
rapidly and radically during the 1960's that it is difficult
to predict with any confidence what is likely to occur during the 1970's. But it appears that future developments—
at least as they relate to the underrepresented minorities—
will take the following forms.

Minority enrollment (and especially that of Black
Americans) will continue to increase steadily during the
next decade, but it is not likely to grow rapidly enough
to satisfy the more vocal and militant. Black enrollment
probably will not reach, by 1980, the point at which the
ratio of black students to total enrollment equals the ratio
of all blacks to the total population. Other minorities will
be even more poorly represented. Continued growth of
white, lower-middle-class enrollment will make it almost
impossible for the minorities to "catch up" within a decade.

Current enrollment patterns (i.e., attendance at certain
types of institutions) are likely to continue and may become even more pronounced. The public sector will grow
more rapidly than total enrollment, and the public two-

year college will continue to be the fastest-growing type of institution. Virtually all of the growth of minority enrollment will be in historically non-black colleges. Traditionally black institutions (and especially those under private control) may well experience an absolute decline in enrollment.

There will be increased militancy displayed by, and more attention paid to, the smaller minorities—Mexican Americans, Puerto Ricans, and American Indians. Almost all the problems encountered by higher education in dealing with Black Americans will be more acute when colleges try to improve their services for the other underrepresented minorities.

Increasingly, public attention and concern are likely to shift from "the disadvantaged" and "racial minorities" to "the poor." Lower-middle-class whites thus far have been surprisingly quiet while militant racial and ethnic minorities have been making substantial gains. This probably will change, and poor whites may be expected to flex their muscles. A major question is whether relatively new *economic class* ties will prove to be stronger than long-standing *racial caste* divisions. Much depends, of course, on the economic health of the country and the availability of jobs. If competition between poor whites and the racial minorities for employment and status intensifies during the 1970's, the educational and civil rights gains of the 1960's may be placed in jeopardy. Low-income whites substantially outnumber poor Black Americans, Mexican Americans, Puerto Ricans, and American Indians, and they have considerable voting strength.

Public funds for higher education probably will increase, but it is doubtful that they ever will match expectations and declared needs. Some form of individual aid embodying the voucher principle is possible. This might be of some help to the private sector of higher education, but it is not likely to encourage very many minority students to enroll in private institutions. Any substantial expansion of federal support of higher education is likely to further diminish and blur distinctions between the public and private sectors.

Institutions of higher learning will continue to change rapidly. Reforms initiated in the last five years are only beginning to gain momentum, and further changes in administration, pedagogy, curriculum, and institutional purpose seem inevitable. It is likely that the net result of these changes will be to make colleges and universities more flexible and more hospitable to minority students.

There will be need for much more analysis and evaluation of higher education's functions, including those that most closely relate to minorities. As higher education increasingly comes to be considered a necessity for all, it increasingly will be held to public accountability. Enrollment and other vital educational statistics probably will be refined and better reported. Longitudinal studies about "high-risk" students and others receiving special educational assistance may be required. There probably will be increased efforts to measure "value added" by the educational process—that is, to determine with some precision the extent to which marginally prepared students benefit intellectually and economically as a result of various types of college training. It is possible that there will be pressure from many quarters to develop rudimentary "cost-effectiveness" measures of higher education's productivity.

The major crunch of the future is likely to be at the point of entry to the labor market rather than at the college door. College is the means, not the end. Right now it is the demand for better jobs and thus better standards of living that drives people (and especially the minorities and the poor) into higher education. Failure of pots of gold to appear at the end of the college rainbow undoubtedly will generate wrenching social tensions. As things now stand, the ones most likely to suffer and to react will be the minorities.

NOTES

1. The 53rd Annual Meeting (October 7-9, 1970, at St. Louis, Mo.) of the prestigious American Council on Education selected as its theme "Higher Education for Everybody?" Although the title was expressed as a question rather than a statement, virtually all of the program participants assumed the inevitability of universality and spoke of the accommodations needed to achieve that end.

2. A recent and rather complete listing of American collegiate institutions and enrollment may be found in *Education Directory, 1969-1970: Higher Education* (Washington, D.C.: U.S. Department of Health, Education, and Welfare, Office of Education, No. HE 5.250:50000-70). See pp. 1-16 for information about the difficulties encountered in trying to classify students and institutions.

3. A useful recent report is *The Social and Economic Status of Negroes in the United States, 1969* (Washington, D.C.: BLS Report No. 375; Current Population Reports, Series P-23, No. 29). The complete 1970 U.S. census figures and reports were not yet available when this analysis was written.

4. During the late 1960's, changes in personnel, procedures, and policies within the Office for Civil Rights made it difficult, if not pointless, to try to determine national minority-enrollment trends by using their data.

5. Reports are available for entering freshman classes in 1966, 1967, 1968, 1969, and 1970. See *ACE Research Reports:* Vol. 2, No. 1-1967 for 1966 freshmen; Vol. 2, No. 7-1967 for 1967

freshmen; Vol. 3, No. 1–1968 for 1968 freshmen; Vol. 4, No. 7–1969 for 1969 freshmen; and Vol. 5, No. 6–1970 for 1970 freshmen. All are published by the Office of Research, American Council on Education, Washington, D.C.

6. *The Social and Economic Status of Negroes in the United States, 1969,* p. 11.

7. See Philip M. Hauser, "Demographic Factors in the Integration of the Negro," in Talcott Parsons and Kenneth B. Clark, eds., *The Negro American* (Boston: Houghton Mifflin, 1966), pp. 71–101.

8. *We the Black People of the United States* (Washington, D.C.: Bureau of the Census, Doc. 1970–0–381–331).

9. Thomas P. Carter, *Mexican Americans in School: A History of Educational Neglect* (New York: College Entrance Examination Board, 1970), provides useful background information about the pre-collegiate educational problems of this group.

10. Edward H. Spicer, *A Short History of the Indians of the United States* (New York: Van Nostrand Reinhold, 1969).

11. Alvin M. Josephy, Jr., *The Indian Heritage of America* (New York: Alfred A. Knopf, 1968).

12. W. Vance Grant, "A Statistical Look at Education in the United States," in *American Education,* VI, No. 8, October 1970 (Washington, D.C.: U.S. Department of Health, Education, and Welfare, Office of Education). Mr. Grant writes, "Approximately 7.6 million students are enrolled in degree-credit programs in institutions of higher education this fall. This represents an increase of about 4 per cent over the 7.3 million students enrolled in the fall of 1969. The figures for both years exclude approximately 600,000 undergraduates enrolled in occupational or general studies programs which are not creditable toward a bachelor's degree." That would make his 1970 estimated total 8.2 million students. The figure here used (8,050,000) is nearly 2 per cent less than Grant's most inclusive estimate. The major question concerns the numbers of students taking courses that *might* be creditable toward baccalaureate degrees.

13. *The Social and Economic Status of Negroes in the United States, 1969,* p. 53.

14. *School Enrollment in the United States: 1969; Advance*

Data, October 1969 Survey (Washington, D.C.: U.S. Bureau of the Census, Current Population Reports, Population Characteristics, Series P–20, No. 199, April 22, 1970). See also *The New York Times,* October 11, 1970.

15. The initiation of "open admissions" in 1970 at the multi-campus City University of New York (CUNY) had a significant impact on Puerto Rican enrollment. In 1962, only 2 per cent of CUNY freshmen were black or Puerto Rican; in 1970, the figure was about 33 per cent—out of more than 35,000 freshmen! It is possible that CUNY's total 1970 enrollment of about 195,000 includes two-thirds to three-quarters of the estimated total national enrollment of 20,000 Puerto Ricans. *Time,* XCVI, No. 16 (October 19, 1970); *The New York Times,* October 12, 1970.

16. For general background, see "The Negro in Education," in Harry A. Ploski and Roscoe C. Brown, Jr., eds., *The Negro Almanac* (New York: Bellweather Publishing Co., 1967), pp. 477–537.

17. John Hope Franklin, *From Slavery to Freedom: A History of Negro Americans* (New York: Random House, 1967), pp. 202–4.

18. Leslie H. Fishel, Jr., and Benjamin Quarles, eds., *The Negro American: A Documentary History* (New York: William Morrow, 1968), p. 157.

19. A useful summary is Henry Allen Bullock, *A History of Negro Education in the South* (Cambridge, Mass.: Harvard University Press, 1967).

20. Dwight O. W. Holmes, *The Evolution of the Negro College* (College Park, Md.: McGrath Publishing Co., 1934), p. 9.

21. Elias Blake, Jr., "Background Paper on the Traditionally Negro College." (An unpublished paper presented by the National Association for Equal Opportunity in Higher Education to the Special Subcommittee on Education, U.S. House of Representatives, February 25, 1970.)

22. Franklin, *op. cit.,* p. 550.

23. Holmes, *op. cit.,* p. 160.

24. *Ibid.,* p. 185.

25. *Ibid.,* pp. 186–90.

26. Franklin, *op. cit.,* p. 551.

27. *Ibid.,* p. 550.

28. Hauser, *op. cit.,* p. 73. It should be noted that the South, as defined by the Bureau of the Census, includes Maryland, Delaware, West Virginia, Kentucky, Oklahoma, and the District of Columbia in addition to the eleven states that comprised the Confederacy.

29. *The Social and Economic Status of Negroes in the United States, 1969,* p. 3. Also see *The New York Times,* October 19, 1970, for preliminary 1970 census returns describing the demography of the South.

30. For a brief description of this population trend and its implications, see chap. 6, "The Formation of the Racial Ghettos," in the *Report of the National Advisory Commission on Civil Disorders*—commonly called "The Kerner Report" (New York: Dutton, 1968), pp. 236–51.

31. *The Social and Economic Status of Negroes in the United States, 1969,* p. 7.

32. A recent analysis of interest is John Egerton's *State Universities and Black Americans: An Inquiry into Desegregation and Equity for Negroes in 100 Public Universities* (Atlanta: Southern Education Reporting Service, 1969).

33. Dorothy M. Knoell, *People Who Need College: A Report on Students We Have Yet to Serve* (Washington, D.C.: American Association of Junior Colleges, 1970).

34. E. F. Schietinger, *Fact Book on Higher Education in the South: 1968* (Atlanta: Southern Regional Education Board, 1968), p. 41. In 1963 in the fifteen states comprising the SREB constituency, a study of black collegiate enrollment showed that 91.3 per cent (95,241 out of 104,286) were enrolled in Negro colleges. Only four years later, the Negro college percentage of total black enrollment was reduced to 76.4 (127,388 out of 166,807).

35. The U.S. Office of Education's *Education Directory, 1969– 1970: Higher Education* reported 2,551 higher institutions (p. 16). Of those, 1,079 were public institutions and 1,472 were under private control. It reported that there were 903 institutions (650 public and 253 private) offering at least two, but less than four, years of instruction, and 1,648 institutions (429 public and 1,219 private) offering baccalaureate, professional, and graduate pro-

grams. The estimates here employed for 1970–71 are substantially the same as those reported in the *Directory,* but it has been assumed that about 50 new public two-year colleges were opened in 1970. The numbers of institutions in the various categories are not constant. Each year some colleges close, new ones are founded, and others merge. Two-year junior colleges change their charters and become senior institutions. Private colleges face bankruptcy and are taken over by the public authorities. Extension centers and branch campuses of large universities are divorced from the parent institution and listed as colleges in their own right. Accordingly, it is possible only to estimate the total number of higher institutions at a given time.

36. See *Higher Education and National Affairs* (Washington, D.C.: American Council on Education), XIX, No. 40 (November 13, 1970), 7. Herman B. Smith, Jr., on behalf of the Office for Advancement of Public Negro Colleges, reported a total 1970 enrollment of 103,825 at the 33 public senior TBI's belonging to that organization. This was a 9.08 per cent increase over their combined enrollment in 1969. Smith also reported that there were about 8,000 white students at 25 responding institutions, and that they constituted 11.28 per cent of the total enrollment at those 25 colleges.

37. An early and useful study is Buell G. Gallagher, *American Caste and the Negro College* (New York: Gordian Press, 1966). This work originally was published in 1938 when the author, a white man, was president of black Talladega College in Alabama.

38. Earl J. McGrath, *The Predominantly Negro Colleges and Universities in Transition* (New York: Teachers College Press, Columbia University, 1965).

39. L. Richard Meeth, "The Report on Predominantly Negro Colleges One Year Later," *The Journal of Negro Education,* XXXV, No. 3 (Summer 1966),204–9. Meeth worked with Earl J. McGrath on his widely publicized report of TBI's published in 1965; this article briefly surveys the situation one year after the original report was issued.

40. McGrath, *op. cit.,* p. 3.

41. *The Social and Economic Status of Negroes in the United States, 1969,* p. 53.

42. In preceding pages it was noted that only an estimated 30.7 per cent of all new black freshmen in 1970 enrolled in TBI's. Incomplete but reliable evidence indicates that TBI freshman enrollment may have peaked in 1968 and barely held its own in 1969 and 1970.

43. Typical of these expressions of concern are remarks made by the president of Clark College, Atlanta, Ga. See Vivian W. Henderson, "The Role of the Predominantly Negro Institution," *The Journal of Negro Education*, XXXVI, No. 3 (Summer 1967), 263–73. After 1967 the situation rapidly became more acute. In the late 1960's, the Alfred P. Sloan Foundation supported a project (under the supervision of Robert K. Hage, Director of Financial Aid at Dartmouth College) designed to help privately controlled TBI's strengthen their admissions operations. In an unpublished paper delivered at a TBI admissions seminar in Knoxville, Tenn., on July 8, 1970, Mr. Hage announced that "the 29 colleges which reported on their entering classes had 705 fewer freshmen in 1969 than in 1968. But the most important and striking evidence that we are at least approaching a crisis is that the 30 reporting colleges as a group had 1,668 fewer students than they wanted in last year's entering class!"

44. The Federal Interagency Committee on Education (FICE) reported that 3 per cent (about $120 million out of $4 billion) of total federal funds for higher education in fiscal year 1969 went to TBI's. See *Higher Education and National Affairs*, XIX, No. 27 (August 2, 1970), 4. The combined enrollment of all TBI's is about 2 per cent of national enrollment.

45. The major fund-raising agency representing most of the private senior TBI's is the United Negro College Fund, established during the 1940's. In the late 1960's the public senior TBI's organized an "Office for Advancement of Public Negro Colleges" to publicize the needs of those colleges and attempt to secure increased revenues. In addition, virtually all the TBI's independently try, with varying degrees of success, to raise money from alumni, corporations, and other donors. For an analysis of changing enrollment conditions and their impact on TBI's, see A. J. Jaffee, Walter Adams, and Sandra G. Meyers, *Negro Higher Education in the Nineteen-Sixties* (New York: Praeger, 1968).

46. Some of the factors leading to this situation are described by Thomas F. Pettigrew, "A Sociological View of the Predominantly Negro College," *The Journal of Negro Education*, XXXVI, No. 3 (Summer 1967), 274–85.

47. Joseph H. Fichter, *Graduates of Predominantly Negro Colleges: Class of 1964* (Washington, D.C.: U.S. Department of Health, Education, and Welfare, 1965).

48. An analysis of the Southern situation is contained in: Commission on Higher Educational Opportunity in the South, *The Negro and Higher Education in the South* (Atlanta: Southern Regional Education Board, 1967), pp. 1–4.

49. The black enrollment figure at non-black two-year colleges is extremely difficult to pin down. No doubt many black youth are part-time students; some drop out, re-enter, and extend their enrollment over many years; and many pursue vocational and technical programs which are not designed for senior-college transfer. However, as opportunities at four-year institutions continue to grow and as the competitive necessity for a baccalaureate degree increases, it is likely that a growing proportion of black youth at two-year colleges will enroll in transfer programs and continue their education at senior institutions.

50. T. J. LeMelle and W. J. LeMelle, *The Black College* (New York: Praeger, 1969): "Most black youth go to black colleges because these colleges are almost the only ones receptive to black aspirants" (p. 2). In fact, *most* black youth are not going to TBI's. Those who do, however, probably select TBI's for the reason cited by the LeMelles.

51. Herman B. Smith, Jr., "New Roles for Black Colleges," *Effective Use of Resources in State Higher Education* (Atlanta: Southern Regional Education Board, 1970), pp. 35–39. Also see Henry Allen Bullock, "The Black College Must Turn Black," *ibid.*, pp. 40–42.

52. Christopher Jencks and David Riesman, "The American Negro College," *Harvard Education Review*, XXXVII, No. 1 (Winter 1967), 3–60. For a revised version by the same authors, see "Negroes and Their Colleges," in *The Academic Revolution* (Garden City, N.Y.: Doubleday, 1968), pp. 406–79. This analysis prompted strong objections by TBI spokesmen, who felt it was

an unfair treatment of their institutions and who claimed that the authors were not sufficiently familiar with TBI's and their problems.

53. Louis E. Lomax, *The Negro Revolt* (New York: Harper & Row, 1962). Lomax wrote, "It is often said that Negro colleges are inferior. This, of course, is true" (p. 192). Nevertheless, he continues, "Perhaps the time has come for the Negro revolutionaries to pause and be gracious toward the Negro educators, men who served their time and served it well" (p. 196).

54. Harold M. Rose, "An Appraisal of the Negro Educator's Situation in the Academic Marketplace," *The Journal of Negro Education,* XXXV, No. 1 (Winter 1966), 18–26. Since Rose's article was written, the demand for black educators by non-black institutions has grown in unprecedented fashion.

55. For an outspoken defense of TBI's, see *Harvard Educational Review,* XL, No. 3 (August 1970), 506–11, for a review of four recent books on the subject. The reviewer is Elias Blake, Jr.

56. Included among these were Howard University, by far the largest of the 51, which awards baccalaureate, professional, and graduate degrees and which is considered "private" despite the fact that it receives a substantial proportion of its annual operating revenues directly from federal government appropriations; Atlanta University, which offers only post-baccalaureate instruction and degrees; Meharry Medical College, which features post-baccalaureate programs in health fields; two theological seminaries—Interdenominational Theological Center and Virginia Seminary and College; four institutions which award baccalaureate and some graduate and professional degrees—Fisk University, Hampton Institute, Tuskegee Institute, and Xavier University in Louisiana; and 42 undergraduate colleges.

57. These and the immediately following enrollment figures are for *all* students at the private senior TBI's and are *not* counts of Black American students. The latter constitute, of course, the overwhelming majority of the total TBI enrollment.

58. Henry S. Dyer, "Toward More Effective Recruitment and Selection of Negroes for College," *The Journal of Negro Education,* XXXVI, No. 3 (Summer 1967), 216–29. Dyer recognized that the TBI's needed to strengthen their admissions operations in anticipation of changing enrollment patterns.

59. Many of the 51 private senior TBI's immediately could take better advantage of the short distances that separate one from another. For example, there are six in Atlanta, two in Nashville, two in New Orleans, and two in Columbia, S.C. There are many others with TBI neighbors no more than twenty miles distant.

60. *Public Negro Colleges: A Fact Book* (Atlanta: Office for Advancement of Public Negro Colleges, 1969). It is reported that in 1968–69 the senior public TBI's enrolled 93,470 students (including non-blacks), an increase of 7.7 per cent over the preceding year and double the 1956 figures. The 1970 estimate reported above was 108,000 and assumed annual increases of slightly more than 5 per cent in each of the preceding two years. See note 36 above for 1970 figures from the Office for Advancement of Public Negro Colleges.

61. Richard I. Ferrin, *Barriers to Universal Higher Education* (New York: College Entrance Examination Board, 1970). This study concentrates on the financial, academic, motivational, and geographic deterrents.

62. The College Entrance Examination Board sponsored a colloquium on "Barriers to Higher Education" at Wingspread, Racine, Wisc., on June 24–25, 1970. At this writing the papers delivered at the colloquium are not yet published. The titles of those papers, however, indicate the nature of concern about certain barriers: "Educational Opportunity and the Organization of Higher Education," "Uses and Abuses of Scholastic Aptitude and Achievement Tests," "Are Standardized Test Scores and High School Grades Better Predictors for Regular College Applicants than for Disadvantaged Ones?," "Lack of Money: A Barrier to Higher Education," "Alternatives to Tests of Scholastic Aptitude and Achievement in the Admissions Process," "Open Admissions," "Alternatives to Tests," and "Assessment of Key Programs."

63. B. Alden Thresher, *College Admissions and the Public Interest* (New York: College Entrance Examination Board, 1966). Thresher observes, "Access to higher education is essentially a social process deeply involved with the society's entire cultural pattern and system of values" (p. 3).

64. The Carnegie Commission on Higher Education, *A Chance to Learn: An Action Agenda for Equal Opportunity in Higher Education* (New York: McGraw-Hill, 1970). In a discussion of

barriers, the following point is made: "There are other factors, such as size of family and educational attainment of parents, that influence college attendance, but the five factors most relevant to social policy are income level of family, ethnic grouping, geographic location, age, and quality of early schooling" (p. 3).

65. Claude M. Fuess, *The College Board: Its First Fifty Years* (New York: Columbia University Press, 1950).

66. S. A. Kendrick and Charles L. Thomas, "Transition from School to College," *Review of Educational Research,* XL, No. 1 (February 1970), 151–79. This article surveys much of the recent research on disadvantaged students and their selection for college. It points out: "The question not answered by anyone is precisely *what talents* require *what* program to *what ends*" (p. 158).

67. Milton Schwebel, *Who Can Be Educated?* (New York: Grove Press, 1968).

68. Hansom Prentice Baptiste, Jr., "A Black Educator's View: The Pseudo-Sacrosanct Role of Intelligence in Education," *The Notre Dame Journal of Education,* I, No. 2 (Summer 1970), 122–27.

69. Arthur R. Jensen, "How Much Can We Boost IQ and Scholastic Achievement?" *Harvard Educational Review,* XXIX, No. 1 (Winter 1969), 1–123. In this widely quoted and highly controversial article, Jensen argued that IQ is determined in large measure by genetic as well as by environmental influences. In the succeeding issue of the *Harvard Educational Review* (XXIX, No. 2 [Spring 1969]), there were critical responses to Jensen's article by Jerome S. Kagan, J. McV. Hunt, James F. Crow, Carl Bereiter, David Elkind, Lee J. Cronbach, and William F. Brazziel.

70. The textbook definition is as follows: Standard deviation is the square root of the arithmetic mean of the square of the deviation from the arithmetic mean of a frequency distribution.

71. This observation is not limited to college entrance examinations. See *The Social and Economic Status of Negroes in the United States, 1969,* p. 84. Essentially the same variation between the "white mean" and the "black mean" occurred with the written Armed Forces Qualification Test given to draftees. In 1966, 43 per cent of black draftees and 8 per cent of white draftees "failed"

the test. In 1967 standards were lowered, and as a result the "failure" rate was reduced to 27 per cent of the blacks and 7 per cent of the whites. The point is that the AFQT is measuring the same thing (admittedly at a somewhat different level) as the typical college entrance examination, i.e., the ability to read and write standard English.

72. Note, however, that if this "moderately selective" institution chose to apply some reverse discrimination, and if it accepted only 225 freshmen from among its 1,383 applicants, it could take all 34 minority candidates and only 191 "all others." Thus, it *could* have an entering class in which 15 per cent were minority students. In such an unlikely situation, the result would be that no other high-scoring minority students would be available to the recruiters of other colleges and universities. The institution in this example would have them all!

73. Humphrey Doermann, *Crosscurrents in College Admissions,* rev. ed. (New York: Teachers College Press, Columbia University, 1970). This excellent study should be required reading for all college admissions officers and others concerned with minority access to higher education. In a series of provocative statistical tables, Doermann estimates the numbers of high school graduates in groups categorized by both family income and admission test scores. Generally speaking, there are fewer "high-scoring, low-income" youth than most journalists and propagandists assumed. Particularly discouraging are the figures dealing with black high school graduates.

74. A journalistic attack on objective testing and the general process of rank-ordering is Hillel Black, *They Shall Not Pass* (New York: William Morrow, 1963).

75. Kenneth B. Clark and Lawrence Plotkin, *The Negro Student at Integrated Colleges* (New York: National Scholarship Service and Fund for Negro Students, 1963).

76. Thomas Oakland, "A Rationale for Compensatory Education Programs," *The Journal of Negro Education,* XXXIX, No. 1 (Winter 1970).

77. James B. Conant, *Slums and Suburbs* (New York: McGraw-Hill, 1961). Conant's words clearly are relevant a decade later: "It has been established beyond any reasonable doubt that

community and family background play a large role in determining scholastic aptitude and school achievement. Anyone who thinks they do not simply has not visited widely among American schools" (p. 12).

78. James Coleman, "The Concept of Equality of Educational Opportunity," *Harvard Educational Review,* XXXVIII, No. 1 (Winter 1968): "The difference in achievement at grade 12 between the average Negro and the average white is, in effect, the degree of inequality of opportunity, and the reduction of that inequality is a responsibility of the school" (p. 22). Coleman was the principal author of a 1966 report, *Equality of Educational Opportunity,* published by the U.S. Office of Education. A critical response to that report is Daniel P. Moynihan, "Sources of Resistance to the Coleman Report," *Harvard Educational Review,* XXXVIII, No. 1 (Winter 1968), 23–26.

79. *The Social and Economic Status of Negroes in the United States, 1969,* pp. 50–52.

80. John H. Fischer, "Educational Problems for Segregation and Desegregation," in A. Harry Passow, ed., *Education in Depressed Areas* (New York: Teachers College Press, Columbia University, 1963), pp. 290–97.

81. Henry S. Dyer, "School Factors and Equal Educational Opportunity," *Harvard Educational Review,* XXXVIII, No. 1 (Winter 1968), 38–56. Also see James Bolner, "Defining Racial Imbalance in Public Educational Institutions," *The Journal of Negro Education,* XXXVII, No. 2 (Spring 1968), 114–26.

82. See the annual publication "Student Expense Budgets of American Colleges and Universities." This is a College Scholarship Service Technical Report published by the Educational Testing Service, Princeton, N.J.

83. *The Social and Economic Status of Negroes in the United States, 1969,* p. 16.

84. *Toward a Long-Range Plan for Federal Financial Support for Higher Education* (Washington, D.C.: U.S. Department of Health, Education, and Welfare, 1969). This is the so-called "Rivlin Report." See pp. 5–7 for statistics largely based on Project TALENT, a longitudinal survey sponsored by the U.S. Office of Education.

85. *The Social and Economic Status of Negroes in the United States, 1969,* p. 21.

86. See Doermann, *op. cit.,* pp. 48–49. A study of *all* estimated 121,000 black male high school graduates in 1965 led Doermann to the conclusion that between 4,800 and 8,500 would score higher than 450 on the verbal section of the Scholastic Aptitude Test and also would come from families with annual incomes of $7,270 or more. A later study (see Doermann, "Lack of Money: A Barrier to Higher Education," an unpublished paper delivered at a College Entrance Examination Board colloquium at Wingspread, Racine, Wisc., June 24–25, 1970) of *all* estimated 148,000 black male high school graduates in 1970 revealed that only 3,780 (2.5 per cent) would score 450 or higher on the SAT-V and have family incomes of $7,500 or more. In the 1970 study, if family income levels were completely ignored, only 5,200 (3.5 per cent) of black male high school graduates would score SAT-V 450 or better. According to Doermann, 25.3 per cent of the white males would achieve that score. Of *all* male students scoring 450 or better, 328,800 would be white and 5,200 black—blacks would make up only 1.6 per cent, although they constituted 10.2 per cent of all male high school graduates in 1970.

87. Warren W. Willingham, *Free-Access Higher Education* (New York: College Entrance Examination Board, 1970).

88. Bishop College, a private, senior, traditionally black institution now located in Dallas, Texas, provides one example of rapid enrollment growth after moving from a relatively isolated small town to a large metropolitan area. Within a decade after its move, its enrollment tripled, despite the fact that during the same period it raised admission standards significantly and increased tuition charges substantially.

89. William F. Brazziel, "New Urban Colleges for the Seventies," *Journal of Higher Education,* XLI, No. 3 (March 1970), 169–78.

90. *The Social and Economic Status of Negroes in the United States, 1969,* p. 9.

91. For a recent analysis, see Constance McLaughlin Green, *The Secret City: A History of Race Relations in the Nation's Capitol* (Princeton, N.J.: Princeton University Press, 1967).

92. An interesting study of Chicago more than a generation later is Allan H. Spear, *Black Chicago: The Making of a Negro Ghetto, 1890–1920* (Chicago: University of Chicago Press, 1967).

93. A study of Negro New York between 1890 and 1930 is Gilbert Osofsky, *Harlem: The Making of a Ghetto* (New York: Harper & Row, 1966).

94. Robert A. Dentler, "Northern School Desegregation," in Parsons and Clark, eds., *op. cit.:* "More than two thirds of all the racially segregated schools in the North are located in ten of the largest cities" (p. 474). This statement was based on 1965 data, and the situation was probably more sharply drawn by 1970.

95. James W. Trent and Leland L. Medsker declare that the opening of a public college immediately raises the attendance level from one-third of the college-age youth to one-half for all living within commuting distance. *Beyond High School* (San Francisco: Jossey-Bass, 1968), pp. 26–27.

96. Patricia Gurin and Daniel Katz, *Motivation and Aspiration in the Negro College* (Washington, D.C.: U.S. Department of Health, Education, and Welfare, Office of Education, 1966).

97. Irwin Katz, "Academic Motivation and Equal Educational Opportunity," *Harvard Educational Review,* XXXVIII, No. 1 (Winter 1968), 57–65.

98. A contrary view is expressed by Aaron Antonovsky, "Aspirations, Class and Racial-Ethnic Membership," *The Journal of Negro Education,* XXXVI, No. 4 (Fall 1967), 385–93.

99. It is difficult to determine to what extent parental models themselves are motivators. Conrad Taeuber, Associate Director of the U.S. Bureau of the Census, made the following statement in an unpublished paper, "Americans in the 1970's," delivered on October 9, 1969, at a meeting of the Rocky Mountain College Placement Association: "A survey in 1967 found that 47 per cent of the high school seniors in October 1965 had enrolled in college by February 1967. The education of the father was a major factor in the college enrollment of children. Eighty-two per cent of the high school seniors whose fathers had a college education enrolled in college. If the father had less than eight years of schooling, only 22 per cent of the high school seniors had enrolled in college."

100. E. Franklin Frazier, *The Negro Family in the United*

States, revised and abridged ed. (Chicago: University of Chicago Press, 1966).

101. Impressive exceptions are the reports issued by The National Advisory Commission on Civil Disorders (the Kerner Commission) and The President's Commission on Campus Unrest (the Scranton Commission). The latter, in chap. 3, "The Black Student Movement," of its report released in October 1970, comments: "We wish to call attention to the fact that as a nation, we are *now* and *always have been* two societies. Segregation and discrimination, whether *de facto* or *de jure,* have served to keep America's Black citizens in a condition of economic disadvantage, cultural exclusion, social ostracism, political disenfranchisement, and educational inequality." See *The Chronicle of Higher Education,* V, No. 2 (October 5, 1970).

102. John Hope Franklin and Isidore Starr, eds., *The Negro in Twentieth Century America* (New York: Random House, 1967).

103. Thomas F. Pettigrew, "Race and Equal Educational Opportunity," *Harvard Educational Review,* XXXVIII, No. 1 (Winter 1968), 66–76.

104. St. Clair Drake, "The Social and Economic Status of the Negro in the United States" (pp. 3–46), and John Hope Franklin, "The Two Worlds of Race: A Historical View" (pp. 47–68), in Parsons and Clark, eds., *op. cit.*

105. Virgil A. Clift, "Educating the American Negro," in John P. David, ed., *The American Negro Reference Book* (Englewood Cliffs, N.J.: Prentice-Hall, 1966), pp. 360–95.

106. Harold Cruse, *The Crisis of the Negro Intellectual* (New York: William Morrow, 1967).

107. See the *Report of the National Advisory Commission on Civil Disorders* ("The Kerner Report") for descriptions of these riots and comments about their causes.

108. Edmund W. Gordon and Doxey A. Wilkerson, *Compensatory Education for the Disadvantaged* (New York: College Entrance Examination Board, 1966): "The eight Ivy League and Seven Sisters colleges admitted 468 Negro men and women to their freshman classes in the fall of 1965, more than double the number admitted in the previous fall and about 3 per cent of total ad-

missions" (p. 136). It is likely that these selective private colleges were enrolling proportionately more minority students than most of the other private non-Negro higher institutions at that time.

109. The National Scholarship Service and Fund for Negro Students (NSSFNS), founded shortly after World War II, was one of the few agencies that for years before 1968 tried to bridge the gap between black high school graduates and white colleges and universities. It worked diligently and successfully to acquaint guidance counselors and admissions officers with the problems and capabilities of minority high school graduates. Before 1968, however, the black students served were relatively small in number, and most probably were above-average academic performers from black middle-class families.

110. This activity was not limited to a handful of "name" universities by any means. A survey of 129 public and private senior colleges in the Midwest revealed that minority freshman enrollment increased 25 per cent in 1969 over the previous year, and an additional 30 per cent in 1970. It should be noted, however, that in 1968 minority freshmen represented 3.7 per cent of the combined 129 freshman classes, 4.5 per cent in 1969, and 5.6 per cent in 1970 ("Admission of Minority Students in Midwestern Colleges," prepared by Warren W. Willingham [Report M–1, Higher Education Surveys], New York: College Entrance Examination Board, May 1970). Also see John Egerton, op. cit.

111. The Ford Foundation made 55 grants between May 15, 1968, and July 21, 1970, in support of a variety of efforts to lower the barriers to higher education. Twenty-five of these grants went to individual institutions to help them initiate programs of recruitment and "special handling" of Black Americans, Mexican Americans, Puerto Ricans, and American Indians. Many of the observations that follow are based on the experience of those 25 colleges and others with similar programs. The Foundation, during those two years, made hundreds of additional grants relating to educational and other problems of minorities.

112. Doermann, *Crosscurrents in College Admissions*, pp. 48–49, 159–62.

113. John Egerton, *Higher Education for "High-Risk" Students* (Atlanta: Southern Education Reporting Service, 1968).

114. Perhaps the most publicized and most significant policy change was made by the huge, multi-campus, public City University of New York (CUNY), which inaugurated "open admissions" in the fall of 1970. A one-year increase in the size of the combined freshman classes from 20,000 to 36,000 also changed the percentage of minority freshmen from about 22 to 33. Under the new arrangement, CUNY offered some form of admission to any New York City high school graduate, regardless of prior academic record, admission test scores, or type of high school program completed. Before the policy change, CUNY (in some of its divisions, at least) had been quite selective at the point of admission.

115. Vice-President Spiro T. Agnew, at Des Moines, Iowa, on April 13, 1970, spoke of "the disturbing trends in administrative and admissions policies of America's colleges and universities." He said, in part: "When decisions begin to represent a definite trend that may drastically depreciate [our higher institutions], then all of us have an interest at stake. . . . Preparatory and compensatory education do not belong in the university. Students needing special educational services—who do not meet the standards and requirements of higher education—should not be encouraged to apply—in the first instance—to such institutions. . . . A firm commitment to equality of opportunity must not result in the dilution of that opportunity. For colleges and universities to deliberately draw into a high academic environment students who are unqualified intellectually or whom the primary and secondary schools have conspicuously failed to prepare is to create hopes which are doomed to disappointment. . . . College, at one time considered a privilege, is considered to be a right today—and is valued less because of that. . . . It should be our objective to find, to nurture and to advance that natural aristocracy through the rigorous demands of intellectual competition." For responses and reactions to Mr. Agnew's speech by eighteen educators (including the author of this paper), see *College Board Review*, No. 76 (Summer 1970).

116. It should be noted that all the major testing organizations —the American College Testing Program, the Educational Testing Service, the College Entrance Examination Board, and many others—for years have been experimenting, developing new tests,

and seeking new measuring devices for use with minority students.

117. The Carnegie Commission on Higher Education, *Quality and Equality: New Levels of Federal Responsibility for Higher Education* (New York: McGraw-Hill, 1968).

118. There were some noteworthy exceptions to this policy, however. The Ford Foundation inaugurated four large programs of individual aid for minority students between 1968 and 1970. These were designed not for entering minority freshmen but for advanced and graduate students who planned to embark on academic careers in higher education. These awards were made to individuals, who then were free to choose the institutions they wished to attend.

119. Gordon and Wilkerson, *op. cit.:* "A substantial number of institutions of higher education are attempting through a variety of approaches to help socially disadvantaged young people who could not otherwise do so to enter and succeed in college" (p. 153). The authors further point out, "Most of [these approaches] seem to fit the somewhat dreary pattern of remedial courses which have plagued generations of low achieving students with but little benefit to most of them. . . . Very few of the compensatory programs in higher education have been systematically evaluated" (p. 155). These observations, made two years before the King murder, still appear to be true.

120. David Mallery, *Ferment on the Campus* (New York: Harper & Row, 1966). This early report gives clues about the more serious troubles yet to come.

121. See the *Report of the President's Commission on Campus Unrest* ("The Scranton Report"). In *The New York Times* of September 27, 1970, the Commission was quoted as follows: "Campus protest has been focused on three major questions: war, racial injustice, and the university itself. The first issue is the unfulfilled promise of full justice and dignity for blacks and other minorities. Blacks, like many others of different races and ethnic origins, are demanding today that the pledges of the Declaration of Independence and the Emancipation Proclamation be fulfilled now. Full social justice and dignity—an end to racism, in all its human, social and cultural forms—is a central demand of today's students, black, brown, and white."

122. Harry Edwards, *Black Students* (New York: Free Press, 1970).

123. Marvin Bressler, "White Colleges and Negro Higher Education," *The Journal of Negro Education*, XXXVI, No. 3 (Summer 1967), 258–65.

124. Melvin Drimmer, ed., *Black History: A Reappraisal* (Garden City, N.Y.: Doubleday, 1968).

125. Frank H. Bowles, *Access to Higher Education: The International Study of University Admissions* (New York: UNESCO, 1963).

126. Earl J. McGrath, ed., *Universal Higher Education* (New York: McGraw-Hill, 1966).

127. Doermann, *Crosscurrents in College Admissions*, pp. 48–49.

128. Institute for Higher Educational Opportunity, *A Unitary State System of Higher Education* (Atlanta: Southern Regional Education Board, 1970). This report warns that "by 1975 there will be about two and a half million students in colleges in the South, with two million of these in public institutions. This is almost 700,000 more students than are enrolled today. Much of this increase will come because more black students will go to college. . . . If the goal of equal opportunity for higher education is to be reached, new planning must occur within a framework of criteria which are educationally oriented and operationally sound." See also Willingham, *Free-Access Higher Education*, for information about the need for state planning to better serve growing population centers.

INDEX

133

Quotas for admission, 17

Racial barrier, 74-75
Racial statistics, value of, 7-9
Reservations, number of Indians on, 12
Riots, 4, 79-80, 95
Rochester, N.Y., disorders in, 79

St. Augustine Fla., disorders in, 79
St. Louis, Mo., percentage of Black Americans in, 68, 69
San Antonio, Tex., percentage of Black Americans in, 69
San Diego, Calif., percentage of Black Americans in, 69
San Francisco, Calif., percentage of Black Americans in, 69
Savannah, Ga., disorders in, 79
Seattle, Wash., percentage of Black Americans in, 69
Segregation, erosion of, 32-33
Slavery, 26
Social mobility, collegiate credentials and, 4
South, the, decline of Black Americans in, 31
Southern Regional Education Board, xii
Standard deviation (S.D.), 57
Student, interpretation of the term, 6

Tampa, Fla., disorders in, 79
Teachers, number of, 3-4

Technical institutes, 6
Test barrier, 55-61
Texas, Mexican Americans in, 11
Theological seminaries, 6
Trade schools, 6
Traditionally black institutions (TBI's), xi-xiii, 36-42
academic quality, 40-41
administration, 40
black private colleges, 43-49
curriculum, 45-46
enrollment, 43-49
number of, 43, 46-48
size of, 45-48
Bureau of the Census on, 38
compared to all other institutions, 41
competition from all other institutions, 42
curriculum, 40
enrollment, 36-42
whites, 37-38
future opportunities, 40
lack of white support for, 41
need for change in, 42
number of, 36-37
sources for funds, 39
student distribution, 33-35
Tuskegee Institute, 46
Two-year colleges, 71
increase in enrollment 32

U.S. Bureau of Education *Bulletin,* 28-29
Universities, number of, 3-4

Washington, D.C., percentage of Black Americans in, 68